Say It and Solve It

Get the results you want from the business conversations that count

Karl James

PEARSON

Harlow, England • London • New York • Boston • San Francisco • Toronto • Sydney
Auckland • Singapore • Hong Kong • Tokyo • Seoul • Taipei • New Delhi
Cape Town • São Paulo • Mexico City • Madrid • Amsterdam • Munich • Paris • Milan

Pearson Education Limited
Edinburgh Gate
Harlow CM20 2JE
United Kingdom
Tel: +44 (0)1279 623623
Web: www.pearson.com/uk

First published 2014 (print and electronic)
© Karl James 2014 (print and electronic)

The right of Karl James to be identified as author of this work has been asserted by him in accordance with the Copyright, Designs and Patents Act 1988.

Pearson Education is not responsible for the content of third-party internet sites.

ISBN: 978-0-273-79175-1 (print)
       978-0-273-79463-9 (PDF)
       978-0-273-79464-6 (ePub)
       978-1-292-00815-8 (eText)

British Library Cataloguing-in-Publication Data
A catalogue record for the print edition is available from the British Library

Library of Congress Cataloging-in-Publication Data
James, Karl, 1963-
 Say it and solve it : get the results you want from the business conversations that count / Karl James.
    pagings cm
 Includes bibliographical references and index.
 ISBN 978-0-273-79175-1
 1. Business communication. 2. Conversation. 3. Communication in organizations. I. Title.
 HF5718.J26 2014
 650.101′4--dc23
                              2014013090

10 9 8 7 6 5 4 3 2 1
17 16 15 14

Text design by Design Deluxe

Cover design by Two Associates

Print edition typeset in 9.5pt Mundo Sans by 30
Printed edition printed and bound in Great Britain by Henry Ling Ltd., at the Dorset Press, Dorchester, Dorset

NOTE THAT ANY PAGE CROSS REFERENCES REFER TO THE PRINT EDITION

Say It and
Solve It

CONTENTS

ABOUT THE AUTHOR

After fifteen years specialising in conversation and dialogue, Karl's expertise in his field is now widely recognised. As director of The Dialogue Project, founded by Karl in response to the events of September 11th 2001, he spends most of his time enabling powerful and purposeful conversations, bringing together people with different points of view to help them to cocreate ideas and solutions.

Evidence of Karl's work can be found in a wide range of workplaces: from the board room of global giants like Unilever to the classrooms of primary and secondary schools across the UK. A trusted advisor, practitioner, facilitator and negotiator, his client list includes British Airways, British Telecom, Tesco Bank, Pizza Express, McKinsey & Co., and No. 10 Downing Street. But Karl also prides himself on working with less well-known, innovative organisations like The Green Alliance, The Architectural Association, We Are Friday, Arrival Education and Educare Small School in Kingston. Karl created and facilitated Your Thoughts With Mine, a series of conversations between members of Muslim communities in the UK and his series *Intimate Conversations* found a home in the woods for Latitude Festival's first five years. His debut broadcast on BBC Radio 4, *A Different Kind of Justice*, was a critical and popular success and has been nominated for a Radio Academy Award in 2014 while his ongoing series of podcasts: 2+2=5 attracts a loyal and growing audience every month.

In his spare time, Karl co-directs the plays of Tim Crouch with Andy Smith, most recently *Adler & Gibb* at the Royal Court Theatre in London. But when he's not working Karl most enjoys just being at home with his wife Holly and enjoying the challenges of trying to be a good dad to his three sons Billy, Stanley and Albert.

You can find out more about Karl and The Dialogue Project in a number of different places:

Twitter: @2plus2makes5

Website: www.thedialogueproject.com

Blog: www.understandingdifference.blogspot.com

Podcasts: http://bitly.com/2plus2makes5_thepodcasts

THANKS

This book is possible only because of the many people who've taught me what I know so far. And I feel deeply obliged to all of them.

First, my thanks and acknowledgements go to the people who are experts in the field of conversation.

The first two names I must mention are Gerry Egan and Andrew Bailey, who introduced me to the rigour and language of dialogue, ably assisted by the tirelessly optimistic Peter Osborn.

With barely a breath between them though, I need to pay tribute to the great Rod Wright, who inspired and encouraged me towards my own iteration of the core skills. My language around those skills may have changed in the years since my time working with Rod, but the whole-hearted intention we shared to connect with others and understand difference remains intact. The practice of those skills with the thousands of people I've encountered and connected with since Rod's untimely death is one small but significant living signature of his legacy. Thank you, Rod.

To the great Bill Isaacs, whose brilliant book *Thinking Together* first really captured my imagination in the field of dialogue, thank you for being such a thoughtful and brilliant writer. This book is certainly no attempt to compete with your intellect. I'll just carry on trying to make things as practical as I can, inspired as I am by your principles and thinking.

And thanks, of course, to my erstwhile coworkers Julie Batty and David Kershaw, whose voices and minds have long been invaluable sources of ideas and refinements. Huge thanks to Dave Lewis at Unilever, who could so easily have cancelled a project called Braver Conversations on his arrival in his new post, but instead agreed to record a conversation with me and in doing so initiated a long-lasting, ongoing series of powerful, authentic conversations between us. My deepest and heartfelt recognition to Alan Walters, who has learnt never to refuse the bravest conversations of all; you'll continue to inspire many people, Alan, me included, long after we hit the record button for the last time. Thanks, too, to Beth-Marie Bristow, Katherine Mellor and Alastair Creamer at Project Catalyst, who trusted my instinct, even before I knew what I was talking about; and to Camilla Harrisson, who has been ever ready to support my work and always believed I could write a book, even when I didn't. To you all, thank you.

My own working life is full of good conversations, the best of which have been with my dear friends Andy Smith and Tim Crouch. Dear men, both, thank you for your confidence, your support, your honesty and your inspiration. Don't ever stop challenging me to think harder.

My gratitude to my long-suffering agent, Zoe King and Liz Bonsor at The Blair Partnership and of course to Eloise Cook, Natasha Whelan and the wonderful editing and design team at Pearson. A graceful nod to Sam Jackson, who long ago first said yes to the idea of me writing a book of some sort. Even if it wasn't this one.

I thank my two sons, Billy and Stan, whose tolerance I have tested beyond what's reasonable and fair. (But who both need to Listen to their father more than they do.) I treasure the conversations we've had along the way so far almost as much as I look forward to the ones yet to come. I thank my Mum, for telling me to ask good questions every day and for walking the talk.

And I can't even begin to find the right words to thank my beautiful wife, Holly, who has patiently tolerated more late nights than I care to mention and who remains a quiet, gentle, kind and calm presence in my rejuvenated life.

And, finally, to everyone I've ever recorded a conversation with: your part in helping me to understand what does and doesn't work in a conversation is a unique and extraordinary source of information for me. With every edit, with every listening back to the conversations we've had, I *learn* more and more; not just about you, but about myself. For your honesty, your questions, your thoughtfulness and your time, I thank you.

I hope you enjoy the book.

INTRODUCTION

At work, as in the rest of our life, some conversations are more important than others.

And this book is about how to improve the conversations that really count.

How to solve the tough problems by saying first that they exist.

How to say *yes* to having the conversations that tackle the challenges we face at work, that create bold, creative solutions, that enable big decisions and significant choices.

The conversations that *take on* fear and seize opportunities.

The conversations we *have* to have. Because they're not going to go away.

And the conversations we care about. Because the stakes are higher than normal.

These are the conversations of consequence, the conversations that can change, shape and influence our work.

The conversations that sort things out.

Conversations like this can be amazing. They can feel exciting, exhilarating and empowering. But because there *are* consequences to these conversations, sometimes they can also feel a little bit scary. And, like most scary things, we sometimes need a bit of help to do them.

(Sometimes accepting that we need help is hard. But it's the first step towards change. So do it.)

You can do it

The first thing I want you to know is that you more than likely have what it takes to have any conversation. You just don't know it yet.

The reason I feel confident enough to say that is that, having worked on and with the subject of conversations when the stakes are high for more than 15 years now, in essence I've learnt just two important things.

First – we *all* have conversations we're scared of. The boldest and the brightest of us have our Achilles heel. I'm thinking of the teacher who's brilliant at talking and listening to her pupils in the classroom, but who goes home and finds it almost impossible even to start a conversation with her partner who's depressed and non-communicative. Or the brilliant chief executive who runs a huge organisation and is capable of charming apparently anyone, but who's stiff with shyness when it comes to talking to his teenage daughter.

So, if you're thinking, "Why is it *so* hard for me to talk to *this* person?" or to have 'that' particular type of conversation, take heart. You're not alone. Conversational confidence in one setting certainly doesn't guarantee it elsewhere. We're all susceptible. And none of us is beyond a bit of support sometimes.

The second thing I've realised is (I hope) equally encouraging and it's this: it doesn't take much effort to make a big difference when it comes to having a successful big conversation.

If we care enough to learn just a few new things, if we can stretch ourselves just a little, it's possible to influence how well our conversations go at work more than we might think. I've seen people – ordinary people – handle incredibly high-stakes conversation in ways they would *never* have believed themselves capable of. And they've not had to go on a deep spiritual journey, or spend years in therapy to do it. They've simply stopped for a while to think, to consider, to reflect – and learn a few simple skills.

But how can we tell when these skills are needed? And how can we tell when a conversation that counts is on the horizon?

Early signs

I've already given you the rational description of what qualifies as a significant conversation. But a long time before our mind gets involved, there are physical symptoms that tell us how much a conversation matters: that slight tension you notice in your stomach maybe; a sudden change in your body temperature; an uncomfortable warm flush that creeps up the back of your neck. The body gives us an intuitive sense that the conversation we need to have is a significant one. And that fundamental human instinct kicks in: fight or flight. We run like hell and avoid it completely or put up our metaphorical fists and start swinging..

If the fight instinct wins the day, we can find ourselves crashing into a conversation in an uncontrolled way. We jump into confront mode, risking (and sometimes creating) a difficult, painful or upsetting experience. We say things we don't mean. We jeopardise a big meeting. We give ourselves a whole load of new problems to contend with. We demotivate colleagues. Or give a client the wrong impression. And we'll hate ourselves for doing it.

Or, more likely, survival instinct kicks in and we flee the risk. The conversation we know we *ought* to have is left un-had and our feelings are left to fester. Important decisions get put off *again* and problems remain problems. (Or become bigger ones.)

Well, I have some good news.

It doesn't have to be like this.

If you can invest a little time to explore what goes on *inside* a conversation that works, you can consciously engage the mind to find enough confidence to handle the fears and take on that conversation. And you don't have to be clever to do it. I know that. Because I'm not clever. I'm practical. And I'm curious. And I've discovered that a few simple things make a big difference.

A bit about me

I've interviewed hundreds of people who've struggled to say what they need to say. Or who've found it completely impossible to listen. I've read, talked and listened to experts from different walks of life for whom conversations that count are part of their daily practice. Chief executives, peace negotiators, cancer surgeons, therapists, people like that. I've sat between people with extreme and different points of view and helped them reconcile what have seemed like irreconcilable differences. People like environmental groups and oil companies, teachers and pupils, husbands and wives.

I've taught people how to handle big and scary conversations for themselves: from grown-ups in government to five-year-olds and teenagers, company directors and waiters, rational and emotional, men and women, old and young. I've enjoyed working with people from many different hues and backgrounds and have helped them get through some big conversations and make significant breakthroughs – just by talking and listening more effectively.

I've also had a few conversations that count in the last few years. With colleagues, suppliers, clients, my ex-wife, my new wife, my children, and my best friends. The rooms and the relationships have changed, but I've trusted the same tools in every situation. And it's worked. Even when it didn't feel like it was working at the *time*, I realised later that the way in which we'd handled a particularly important conversation had a significant and positive effect on the *consequences* of that conversation.

And here's what I've done, nearly every time.

I've trusted and practised 10 essential ingredients of dialogue. Ten simple things to do more often. Ten skills that form the spine of this book. I didn't invent them. But I have mined them, defined them and over time refined them. And I've shared them in workplaces around the world. And just about *every* time I've shared them, they've worked. Not because I'm a conjurer; I've just made a habit out of practice. I've done it lots of times. And I've got better at it.

And now, after 16 years of research and practice, I'm ready to share those skills here, so you too perhaps can feel a similar sense of confidence and maybe even come to agree with me that there truly is *no such thing* as a conversation that *can't* be had.

So at its simplest, this book is a chance for you first to become aware of a few skills and learn more about them in Part 1; and then, as you get into Part 2, begin to think about putting them into practice in work situations.

Three good things

Good conversations feel like action; because they *are* action, so I want the chapters that follow to be an opportunity for you to learn how to *do* some of the practical things that influence how well a conversation can go.

I want to show you where the levers are. I want to illustrate what happens when you pull this or push that. And I want to help you see that just a gentle adjustment at one end can make an important difference at the other. And I want you to know that you can influence the very *hardest* of conversations, even with people who intimidate you or in situations that create tension in you.

Maybe it's a big meeting that you're running. Maybe it's a feedback session. Maybe it's a client meeting, or a situation with your boss that's begging out for the two of you to solve once and for all.

Whatever the context and whatever the subject matter, whatever the *it* is, I want talking about it to help you solve it. I want what follows to help you *have* that conversation that counts. And I want you to come out of that conversation with at least three positive things:

1. *Movement* where there was a feeling of being trapped or stuck.

2. *Satisfaction* as opposed to frustration.

3. *New possibilities* instead of familiar problems.

What do I get out of it?

Let's say you do make the effort. What are the benefits to you and the work you do?

That's easy.

First, you'll save time, money and be happier.

Second, good conversations create change and improve relationships. They get things done. And they combine talents.

Life and work might be simpler if we never had to have big conversations. But, if we want to thrive, if we want to innovate, if we want to grow and learn at work, we need to talk to each other. We need to tackle the tough stuff with our colleagues and build new possibilities with the people we work with. Bosses, team members, suppliers, clients and customers. It's the conversations with these people that get us through the tough situations, help us make the best out of the opportunities that come along. And, by paying attention to the quality of the conversations we have with them, not only do we get somewhere new, we build stronger, better relationships with them.

So – I hope you enjoy your journey into the world of having conversations that count. And that by the time you've finished turning the pages that follow, you at least feel confident enough to know one thing:

No matter how much the conversation counts, you're capable of having it.

Part 1
The Skills

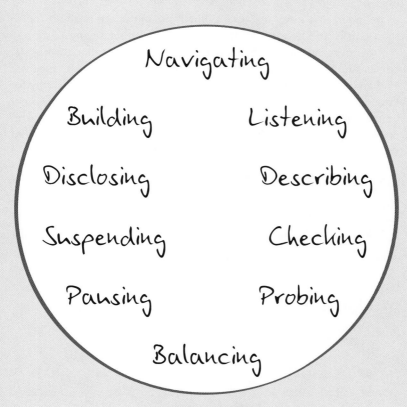

The 10 core skills

Time and Space

When, where and how

It doesn't matter how skilled you are, if the time and place isn't right, you'll struggle to have a decent conversation.

Some examples of this are almost too obvious to mention. Taking on a big subject when you only have 10 minutes is as crazy as trying to be heard in a noisy restaurant. But Time and Space is about more than clocks and geography. It goes almost without saying I'd hope, that of course you need to clear enough time in your diary to have a conversation that counts. But time is about *timing*, too. And it's relative. Half an hour in the morning when you're fresh and have the energy to listen is a very different thing to sitting down late in the afternoon when you're carrying the burden of a long and stressful day. So, when you're considering time, it's the quality of your investment in the conversation that makes the difference, not the number of minutes that pass by.

We've all had conversations that are yawn-inducing after just five minutes. But I hope you'll also have experienced the opposite; that sensation of being so totally engaged in a conversation that, when you happen to check your watch, you find you've been talking for much longer than you thought. That's a sign of a great conversation.

(If this hasn't happened to you recently, try putting yourself in some new situations.)

And, when it comes to creating the right *space* for a conversation, it isn't just about booking a room with the right number of flip charts and a bit of feng shui. Of course, the basics are crucial. Some conversations are better suited across a table; some lend themselves more to sitting side by side on a sofa. And these kinds of decisions should be deliberate ones. But a good space is created by more than physical distance. It's also about how much *energy* you're prepared to invest in that 20 minutes or so you spend with someone. And it's your choice to put effort into how you listen and talk with someone that will make him or her feel valued, special even.

So, when you're in a significant conversation with someone, going that extra mile to consider not just the when and the where, but the *conditions* for a conversation can make a big difference to the outcome. And by bothering to make some small but deliberate choices about the quality of how you talk and listen, you're already giving a big signal to your partner in conversation that you care about it and them.

So, think about the environment for your conversation before it starts, and don't be afraid to change it *after* it's started, if things aren't working. A small investment of time and energy will make a big difference.

Here are a few examples of questions to ask before and during a conversation to help you create the right qualities of Time and Space in which to have a conversation that counts.

CHECKLIST

1. Can we really concentrate here? (Or are there too many distractions?)

2. Can we easily hear each other? (Or will the background noise or music make listening difficult?)

3. Do we feel relatively relaxed? (Or are we unhelpfully on edge because of where we are?)

4. Are we able to talk privately here? (Or is there a risk of being overheard?)

5. Have we cleared enough time to talk properly? (Or have we squeezed in 10 minutes when we need an hour?)

6. Are we focused? (Or is something niggling away at us? Something that should be sorted out before we begin?)

7. That table between us, is it helping? (Or getting in the way?)

8. Are we both in a good enough emotional and physical space to talk and listen well? (Or might it be useful to spend a few minutes calming down if we're stressed? Or eating if we're hungry? Or maybe just having a cup of tea to revive us a little bit?)

9. Can we both turn off our phones or at least put them out of sight? (*Not* just put them on silent.)

10. How about we turn that ugly, harsh, overhead light off? And put that nice lamp on instead?

In different ways, large and small, all of these options will affect the environment you create for your conversation.

And here are some useful things to *say*:

MAKING TIME

"Is this a good time for you to talk?"

"How much time have we got? Realistically?"

"How are we doing on energy levels? Fancy an apple?!"

"We have only an hour for this meeting. Let's think. How can we make best use of it?"

"We know this might be a tough conversation. Are we both feeling up to it?"

CREATING SPACE

"Do you feel comfortable talking here? We could move somewhere less open, if you want."

"Where would you like to sit? Facing the window might be a bit distracting."

"I'm feeling a bit uncomfortable here. It's not helping me feel like I can say what I really want to. Can we move over there? It looks a bit more private."

"We feel really spread out. I can't see everyone. Is it okay if we move the chairs and sit, so we can see each other?"

DEDICATION

Just a quick word on something that's not physical, intellectual or even emotional. It's about truly *dedicating* yourself to the person you're talking to and the effect it can have on your conversation. Bill Clinton, apparently, is brilliant at this – at creating a *disproportionate* sense of Time and Space. As President then, and elder statesman now, he finds himself regularly in a room full of people, pumped-up and excited to meet him; to have *their* moment with the man himself. Time is always limited, of course, and his aides will point out the key people he should meet. But, apparently, he pretty much ignores their instructions and stops to talk to as many people as he possibly can. And, more often than not, somehow manages to get round the whole room in an incredibly short amount of time. And, on the way home, so the story goes, everyone he's met – *everyone* he's met – boasts proudly and would swear blind that they talked to him for longer than anyone else in the room. Clinton's not a magician. He can't bend clocks. And he can't create more space in a room than there is. But he has a talent for making people feel special. And he knows that the secret to creating a real sense of Time and Space for people is simple.

Even if it's just for a few moments, *dedicate* yourself to them.

The skills you need

10 things in your toolbox you simply have to have

Right, let's get down to it.

Under the bonnet of any really good conversation is an engine made up of 10 moving parts. I call them skills. You can call them whatever you like: tools, techniques, ingredients. What it comes down to, is that they're the 10 things you can do *more* of to help you have a better conversation when it counts; to say it and solve it.

As you move through this book, it'll become clear, I hope, that individually they work really well as stand-alone skills. But the moment they come into their own – ironically – is when they start working together.

(Don't even worry about that yet. First things first. Let's keep it simple.)

For now, let me introduce each one of them to you individually. Each skill has its own chapter coming up and with any luck, you're going to get to know them well. You'll understand them, become familiar with them and, who knows, you may even begin to think fondly of them as your new friends. But at this early stage, I just want you to know their names and what they do.

First, there are 3 things you should know about these 10 skills.

1. There's no particular order to them. (Except for the first one.)

2. None of them will be new to you. (You just might not know how useful and important they are yet.)

3. You already do some of them. (You just don't know it.) And, the point is, you need to become *aware* of what it is you're doing (and *not* doing), so you can do those things *more often* and at the right *moments* in a conversation.

So, here they are: the 10 skills that form the backbone of this book and are here to help you:

1. **Navigating:** Looking after the journey of a conversation to keep it purposeful, safe and, crucially, *with* someone. (Not at them.)

2. **Listening:** How to notice small things. (That other people might not.)

3. **Describing:** How to help other people understand you. (*Really* understand you.)

4. **Checking:** Making sure you really understand what someone means. (Instead of assuming you do.)

5. **Probing:** Digging a bit deeper, finding out more.

6. **Balancing:** Making sure you have the richest perspective possible. (Looking at things from both sides now.)

7. **Pausing:** Creating time to think.

8. **Suspending:** Having a genuinely open mind. (And keeping it that way.)

9. **Disclosing:** Saying what you really think. (Without upsetting people.)

10. **Building:** Adding to and enhancing someone else's idea. (Rather than suggesting another one.)

Now, with any luck, what you're *not* thinking is: "I have absolutely no idea what any of these mysterious words and phrases are all about." Of course not. In fact, I hope you're thinking the opposite. Something more like: "Wait a minute. These words and phrases are all plainly simple and familiar. And I even *do* some of them sometimes."

Good. That's a great start. And you're probably right. You probably do *do* all of these things. Sometimes.

But familiarity isn't knowledge.

Let me explain what I mean in the form of a question:

How many sides does a 50p coin have? (No cheating.)

Five? Six? Seven?

Confident enough to bet £20 on it? Really?

No?

Don't worry. You're not alone.

You're *familiar* with a 50p, but you don't *know* it very well.

And exactly the same can be said for conversation skills. The difference is, you don't *need* to know how many sides a 50p has, right? So long as it drops into the vending machine and works, who cares?

I'll tell you who cares: someone who's blind. When you think about it, it's obvious. The reason a 50p has seven sides is to distinguish it from any other coin that's made anywhere else in the world. Because of its shape, it's immediately recognisable by touch. Which is handy for most of us, but essential to your daily life if you're not able to see and need to tell the difference between a 2p, a 10p and a 50p by using your fingers, not your eyes.

And the analogy holds. When you're in an important conversation, it can sometimes feel like you're clutching blindly for the right thing to say or the best thing to do. Wishing you knew what the most helpful thing to do might be:

"Should I speak more? Should I be quiet for a bit? I wonder if I can just say what I'm thinking?"

These are the kinds of questions we fumble around with, not knowing what constitutes a good decision or a bad one. And *just* at the moment we need to respond quickly, we're hindered by a lack of confidence and skill. If we're lucky, the worst thing that happens is we stay confused, clutch at straws and scramble our way through. If we're less than lucky, we say or do the wrong thing and inadvertently escalate a bad situation into a worse one.

So – the most important thing this book can do for you right now, is to give you a bit more depth and detail on what the core conversation skills are and an understanding of exactly how they can help you. Because, if you understand them better, when you find yourself in need of them, you'll stand a much better chance of having the confidence to pull out the right *thing* at the right *time* and put those skills to work.

Ready? Good. Let's go.

Chapter 1
Navigating

Taking on the journey

Ever other skill in this book depends on Navigating. So it has to come first.

Essentially, Navigating is about awareness. It is about noticing what's happening in a conversation and acting on it. And in a conversation where there's plenty at stake, without Navigation you can easily and dangerously stray off course, find yourself stranded and even, potentially, out of control. *With* Navigating, it's a different matter entirely. If you pay attention to the health of the conversation, you keep it purposeful, steady and connected and there's no conversation that can't be had.

(By the way, good people Navigate. Bad people manipulate. Be good.)

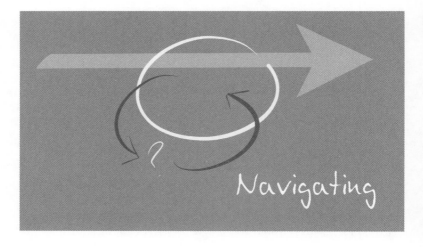

A sense of purpose

I can honestly say that Navigating is the golden key to unlocking conversations at work. And it's partly because it keeps alive the sense of purpose that probably instigated the conversation in the first place. The need was there, so the conversation became necessary. But there's a risk sometimes that, between the need arising and the conversation actually happening, the memory of that need fades. Not, though, if you Navigate.

Let's do a quick list of the good things that can happen if you maintain your sense of purpose:

- Meetings will stay on time.

- Problems will get solved more quickly.

- Decisions will get made more thoroughly.

- Feedback will be given more honestly.

- Ideas and solutions will be more innovative.

- There's less stress and more focus.

- You'll save time, money and energy.

- It'll strengthen relationships between you and the people you work with.

And it's not just about keeping a conversation *purposeful*.

Safety and numbers

Stick together. And stay *safe*. That's pretty good advice for taking on a hard conversation. You need to stay close enough to the person you're having the conversation with to make sure that *wherever* you go, you get there *together*. And the other key aspect of Navigating is to make sure the conversation *stays* safe, in the sense that it doesn't get out of control or drift too far away from where you wanted to be going. That way you don't end up anywhere too dangerous or even just time-wasting. Or, at least if you do, you're *conscious* enough of it to get yourself out of that place.

And to do that – to stay safe and together in a conversation – requires essentially one simple thing: awareness.

Staying aware of the conversation we're having *while* we're having it isn't exactly rocket science. In a way, it's a simple idea but, for a lot of us, it can be a really hard thing to do. Why? Because there are a lot of very human reasons *not* to! Powerful human reasons like emotions, desires and habits.

In a hard conversation, it's easy and very natural sometimes for our emotions to get so involved that our rational side disappears almost completely and we totally lose our ability to step out of the moment we're in. Or we get fixated on what we *want* to happen so much, that we end up chasing it blindly, unaware that the very outcome we're after may not even be possible any more. Or we may even just be so deeply engrained in our habitual ways of talking about something that we don't even notice that in some way we're contributing to the problem rather than finding a solution.

So there's plenty for Navigating to achieve in pretty much any conversation, but especially in a conversation that matters, where the stakes are high.

And Navigating is the right word, too, because it's really about managing the journey of a conversation; from the beginning to the end.

At the *beginning* of a conversation, it's about agreeing three things.

1. *What* we're talking about.

2. *Why* we're talking about it.

3. What *kind* of a conversation we're prepared (and not prepared) for it to be.

As you get into the *body* of a conversation, Navigating's about:

1. Gently "pulling the tiller" when necessary, to keep things on course, adjusting as you go along.

2. Making the most of opportunities and minimising risk.

3. Harnessing the potential of a conversation and maximising its effectiveness.

And then, towards the *end* of the conversation, it's about:

1. Making sure everything's been covered that could have been.

2. Pulling together the outcomes and optimising the value of the conversation.

3. Learning from what's happened here and already looking ahead to the next time.

So, now let's understand more about that core quality that keeps on coming back at us in the context of Navigating: awareness.

And rather than get into too much theory, let's create some examples of Navigating in action and look at some of the different *types* of awareness you're going to need in order to Navigate well.

Awareness of time

When things take too long – or maybe aren't explored long enough – if you Navigate, you can beat the clock before *it* beats *you*. For example:

> **"We said we'd spend only 15 minutes on this subject, guys. We're 20 minutes over that now. What shall we do?"**

Note the use of the word "We"! It's an extremely useful one when it comes to Navigating. It keeps you on the journey *together*.

> **"Okay. We only have 15 minutes left but we still have 3 things on the agenda. On the basis of how we've done so far, it feels to me like they're all going to take about 10 minutes. And we have only 15 minutes left in total. So, how shall we do this? Drop one topic and be tight with the other two? Or go down to one topic, talk about it thoroughly and find another time to finish this properly?"**

What's helpful is that you've noticed how long things are taking in *reality* (not on paper!), you've made some suggestions to save us time thinking about them and then invited everyone else in to make a combined decision.

And, finally, when it comes to time, Listen to how reassuring it is to have someone who's on it, so we can get on with thinking about the content:

> **"Wow! That was quick! Can I just check in with everyone? Have we really covered that area thoroughly enough to move on? If so. . . fine! But we could easily spend five minutes more on it and then take a coffee break..."**

Location, location, location

Now – what about *where* we are? Every good Navigator will have a strong sense of where the journey's taking us:

> **"Hmmm. We're back talking about money again, aren't we? And we had some good reasons why we decided to avoid that until we**

know more about the budget. Do we want to revisit our decision to stay away from it? Or shall we move on to talk about the vision?"

I hope you can see that Navigation isn't about *control*; it's about making visible what's invisible. Calling out a bit of drift when it happens and offering back to everyone involved a choice to do something about it.

As well as noticing when you're in the *wrong* place, there's a lot to be said sometimes for recognition of when you're *exactly* where you said you wanted to be:

"Right. I've heard some outrageous suggestions in the last few minutes, which I seem to remember is precisely what we said we'd try to do. Brilliant! Keep going."

And there's a consciousness, too, not just of what *topic* we're covering, but also of *how* we're covering things:

"We've just done two pretty dry topics back to back. Is there a shorter, maybe a more light-hearted, item on the agenda that might help change gear for us a bit?"

Next up on the awareness spectrum is...

One direction

Working towards a common goal has become such a common phrase in business that it's almost lost its meaning. But when it comes to a conversation that matters, it's a very real idea: aiming to realise a shared ambition or intention; an end point that satisfies everyone's sense of purpose.

And right at the *beginning* of a conversation is when you should Navigate to make this explicit:

"Okay. So, Listening to you all, it sounds like we're talking about this for two main reasons. First – it's an account that's been dropping off steadily, so we need to come up with some big ideas and stop that from happening. And second, this is a business that, potentially, we could look to partner with in future. So, we want to show them our best cards, yes?"

As things move on, it's nearly always worth a reminder of what the central purpose of the conversation is:

> "I wonder if it's worth remembering that what we're trying to do now is come up with a catalogue of ideas. Not to test them too much. We said we'd do that afterwards. Maybe we're fine-tuning too much when we should just be creating more options."

These little nudges in the right direction can save so much time. It's tempting for any number of reasons to get drawn into one kind of activity when you've said you'd focus on another. Navigating is the essential tool when you want to avoid mission creep.

Feeling your way

And then there's the awareness of the emotional temperature in the room that can need adjusting. Sometimes things can get a bit too heated:

> "I can tell there's a lot of hot blood around this subject. People clearly feel passionately about this, which is great. But, there've been a few raised voices now. I think we need as much left brain input as we do right brain. Can I suggest we take a little break? Just so people get a chance to calm down a little bit?"

And sometimes things can get too cool:

> "It feels to me like we're discussing an Excel spreadsheet here. I'm not hearing much gut feel. Is it just me or could we do with a bit more provocation here?"

It's worth saying again that Navigating isn't about manipulating a conversation. It's about picking up on some obvious symptoms; noticing what's apparent to *one* person. And that one person doesn't have to be the boss or arbiter. Their role is simply to bring attention to something, not to be the judge and jury. (Which is why it's a good idea, sometimes, to end with a question that encourages others to put in their perspective, too.)

Outside in

The outside world sometimes will change the conditions for a conversation too, in a way that's worth bringing up:

> "Folks – it's getting a bit noisy outside. I think maybe they've broken for lunch early next door. Are we okay to carry on or is anyone distracted?"

And an awareness of the outside world is as much about spotting opportunities as problems:

> "Can I interrupt briefly? I've just noticed that the sun's come out and it looks so inviting out there. Shall we grab a coffee and go and do half an hour or so outside in the sunshine? Just to break up the morning and maybe refresh our brains a bit?"

Energy

When you're deeply immersed in a conversation, you can be the last to notice that you're getting tired. You might almost be grinding to a painful halt but, especially in a long meeting, it can happen so slowly that there's no one definite moment that breaks the flow. So, if anyone has the awareness to notice that the energy has changed in the room, it's usually a hugely constructive thing to say it out loud:

> "Just looking around the table, I think fatigue might be setting in. I can see on people's faces a slight weariness. And the level of excitement we had an hour or so ago has definitely gone walkabout. Shall we call an emergency tea break?"

Or of course, you can Navigate by noticing something positive about a change in energy, too:

> "Can I just say that there's a very powerful sense of this being important to everyone here. There's an extraordinary atmosphere in the room and I think it might help us enormously to stay with it and hear from a couple more people before we break? What do you think?"

Productivity

Another more subtle form of awareness is not necessarily about the *how* but the *what*. Even if it feels awkward, it's worth noticing out loud if you think there's a drop-off in the effort to outcome ratio. You don't have to have a perfect solution to warrant speaking up. Your role might simply be as the catalyst:

> "I'm going to be honest here and say that we've been thrashing around on this subject for a while now and we're not getting

anywhere. Do you agree? I wonder if there's anything we could be doing differently? Maybe we need to change where we're sitting or... I don't know. Any ideas?"

Pace

Pace and speed are different things. To be made aware of how both are changing can be a hugely helpful thing in a conversation. Sometimes what's working well won't be well known around a table. If you become aware of a pattern or a tendency that's prevalent and you detect a connection between the how and the what, it can be an encouraging spur to do it more.

> "I want to say just briefly: we're covering so much content here. And in such depth. I think it's really helpful that we're being disciplined enough to speak only if we're sure we have something to say. If we keep going like this, we could have time left over at the end to get back to the one thing that we had to postpone yesterday: brilliant stuff."

And of course, you might have to poke people in the ribs occasionally, too, if you notice that time or energy is being wasted:

> "Guys – as entertaining as it is to hear stories that aren't really relevant, I think we should pick up the pace here. We can cover so much more ground if we agree to say only what we've experienced ourselves. Sorry to be blunt, but there's a lot of pontification going on. I'm just trying to help us move through the agenda!"

Key thoughts

1. Navigating is about keeping the conversation purposeful, safe and collective.

2. Awareness is the key. Notice and acknowledge what happens on the journey of the conversation.

3. When you Navigate, your job is not to judge, but to draw attention.

Looking back

There are so many subtleties and nuances to a conversation, I suspect it's actually impossible to imagine being *involved* enough to be fully part of it but, at the same time, *aware* enough to notice everything that's happening in it. Luckily, that's not what you need to do. Ideally, Navigating is a skill to be shared between participants in a conversation. And it takes practice to be good at it. But even when you *are* good at it, you can't notice everything. Oddly, the easiest time to start doing it, is at the end of a conversation. So, start at the end. Next time you've had a hefty conversation, before you part company with your colleague, your client or your boss, take five minutes to look back at the conversation you just had. Review it. Create a little highlights version of it. Reflect on what happened. Exchange thoughts on where it was most enjoyable, least enjoyable, hardest, most exciting or where – if you can put your finger on it – any turning points were. You'll find that simply by looking back, you'll achieve two things: first, you'll learn from what's just happened; second, you'll strengthen your relationship with whoever it was you were talking with. So, look forward to looking back. It's often a surprisingly satisfying and enjoyable thing to do.

Chapter 2
Listening

Navigating

Building

Listening

Disclosing

Describing

Suspending

Checking

Pausing

Probing

Balancing

"You're lucky. Everyone's Listening to you."

OLLY (AGED 7)

Imagine...

That every word you saw...

Every day...

Everywhere...

Imagine...

That every email...

Every document...

Every word in every text on your phone...

In every newspaper...

In every book...

On every Kindle...

Every iPad...

Every poster...

Imagine...

That as you read the words, you see...

They disappear.

For ever.

And that's essentially what Listening is.

That's why Listening is extraordinary.

It's a wonder we're as good at it as we are.

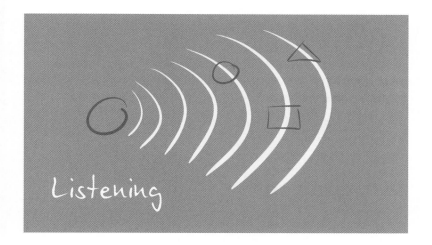

Listening

The quality of our Listening underpins every other conversation skill there is. It's *the* great enabler.

It's present and necessary in so many other aspects of any conversation that counts. How could you Navigate, Check, Probe or Balance without Listening?

Real Listening is so much more than a passive skill. It requires a lot of work. And plenty of looking.

(We Listen with our eyes, as well as our ears after all.)

And in the world of work, great Listening is a rare thing. You can probably count on one hand the people you know that you'd describe as being a really good Listener. But those who *can* and *do* Listen well are amply rewarded by the quantity and quality of what they hear. Great Listeners hear not just what but *why*. They hear context as well as content. They hear clues; small but significant shifts in tone, language, pace and passion.

And if you're a great Listener at work, then you'll be bringing a great deal into your workmates' lives. Listening makes other people feel good about themselves. It helps them open up in new ways. It makes them more articulate. People trust good Listeners. And if you've ever experienced a conversation with someone who is a great Listener, you'll know how good it makes you feel.

So there are many reasons to improve how we Listen. But it's a huge subject! Let's give ourselves a series of lenses through which we can begin to understand how we might Listen better and learn more:

Listening *to*, Listening *for*, Listening *through*, Listening *from* and Listening *with*.

Listening *to*

This is the first kind of Listening we learn to do. As a child we're told to Listen *to* our parents, our teachers and our friends. And as a working adult, we spend most of our time Listening *to* colleagues, clients and customers. It's what we do to search for facts and information, the fundamental and essential benefits of Listening.

None of the more subtle Listening can happen if we can't do the basic thing of hearing properly, which is why it's so intensely annoying when the volume of a microphone is too low, or too loud. Or, indeed, when someone's voice doesn't carry clearly to the back of the room. It's why we enjoy quiet spaces with good acoustics. Many of us won't *know* that's what we're enjoying by the way, but we are. We all appreciate being able to hear clearly and without any sense of strain.

So Listening *to* is about having open access to what's being said. Then it's about what we *discern* from what we hear. The heard word takes us to the idea. The idea is the expression of a shared thought. And it's the skill of Listening *to* that allows us to comprehend that thought and learn from it. At its very simplest, if we Listen *to* someone well, we can begin to *understand* what people are *saying* and what, therefore, they might *mean*.

Now, if we're astute, we'll Listen *to* more than just the words. We'll Listen *to* the spaces between the words, too; the gaps between phrases and sentences that are *so* crucial in allowing us to *absorb* not just *witness* someone speaking. The Pause before (or after) a word radically alters the emphasis on it. We might hear the added weight that's given to a particular phrase. We'll hear the increased pace. The surprising inflection.

The accent of whoever's speaking. There are so many variations in the human voice to which our brain is super alert, if we only it a chance. And the amount of processing that goes on in our minds as we Listen *to* someone is phenomenal. So, if we can optimise the conditions for Listening, if we can make it as easy as possible to Listen *to* whoever's talking, we'll hear so much more.

So, practically, how can we improve this first level of Listening? There are some obvious, but extremely worthwhile things for which we can take responsibility. So many people don't think they can change the conditions for Listening. But you can. In some very simple ways:

1. **Make sure you can see:** Place yourself in a good position in the room where you can *see* the speaker or a screen showing the speaker's face, without anyone or anything in the way.

2. **Make sure you can hear:** Get yourself close enough to the speaker and indeed far enough away from the speaker if it's amplified. If there's a buzz, a distortion or a crackle or anything else wrong with the technology, say so! If someone's not speaking loudly enough – say so! If there's any other background noise, like a busy kitchen, road works or air-conditioning that's interfering with your Listening – say so!

3. **Make sure you're *ready* to Listen:** Make sure you're *physically* ready – not hungry, thirsty or bursting for the loo. Make sure you're *mentally* ready – not distracted by phone calls, texts or emails.

If you want to Listen well, I urge you to be rigorous on these things. People tend to be quick to notice any kind of visual interference and distractions like poor lighting, distracting background or bad-quality projection screens. If you take the initiative on looking after the audio equivalents of these things, you'll not only improve your own ability to Listen, you'll be serving everyone else in the room, too.

Listening *for*

This is where things begin to get a bit more subtle – and powerful. We first learn to Listen *for* when we begin to mature as young people, normally around the age of nine or ten. We begin to pick up information, not just on the *content* but the *context*. We become more conscious of the *how* as well as the *what*. We might notice, for instance, that there's a dissonance between what's being said and how it's being delivered. At a very basic level, we hear Mum telling us to get ready for school, but what we notice is that she seems upset about something.

Some people are more intuitive than others at this kind of Listening. It's a myth, I think, that all girls and women are better than all boys and men. Girls do seem to develop this capacity earlier than boys, it's true. And women are definitely more *intuitive* than their male counterparts in this area. But some of the most sensitive Listeners I know are men. And I certainly know women who aren't good Listeners and who miss what seem to me to be obvious clues that something in the delivery of a message is at odds with the words being spoken.

But let's not deal in generalities. Let's focus on *you* and your capabilities, be you young, old, male or female.

What can we Listen *for* more?

If you really pay attention and *tune in* to someone, you can Listen *for* someone's emotional state, their mood, their frame of mind, their energy. These things will tell you just as much as the content sometimes. It's not a science this, it's a practice. It's something you can learn to do, and do better by doing regularly. If you simply put more effort into your Listening and pay attention to the way things are being said, you'll find there's a seriously wide range of things you can Listen *for*.

We can Listen *for* deeper things than perhaps we're used to hearing. Attitudes. Values. Motivation. Commitment. Beliefs, needs and desires. Different frameworks to our own perhaps, in terms of culture, age, experience and background.

And you can Listen, too, for the *music* of what's being said. The sound. Hear it not so much as a story but as a tune. After a while, you'll begin to hear patterns, repetitions, threads and sonorities in the sound that's being made. You don't need to be a psychoanalyst or an expert in Listening to do it. You just need to trust your human instinct and your ear. And notice when something happens. When something changes.

And when something does happen, when maybe a phrase sticks out for some reason, you don't need to deliver a comprehensive analysis of what it was. All you need to do is surface it. Make it visible. Let me give you three quick and simple examples of how and where Listening *for* like this might prompt you to speak up:

> **"Gosh, your voice changed completely when you talked about your time in Asia."**

> **"I noticed that you Paused for a while, before you answered that question. I wonder what you were thinking then."**

Or:

> **"It feels like you're speaking much more deliberately now."**

In a sense, you've already started to Listen *for* clues, like a detective. I learnt to Listen like this from a rather brilliant man called Dick Mullender, who's a police negotiator. He taught me to get into the habit of Listening forensically like this; Listening for clues. You'll find it an incredibly revealing thing to do. Listen for small things: little moments of hesitation, discomfort. The held breath. The slight catch in the voice. The unexpected mistakes. And again, all you have to do is *notice* these things. Out loud. If you simply state what you've heard you initiate a process of discovery. You reveal what's hidden just beneath the surface. And no matter how small these events are, they might prompt some kind of revelation for the speaker. It's a strange thing, but often people don't hear their own shifts and changes in tone until someone else does, but my experience is that they're often keen to explore them once they've been noticed by someone else:

> **"Did I Pause? How funny. I wasn't aware of that. It was actually quite a difficult time in my career. Maybe that's what you heard."**

Listening *through*

The next stage of Listening is a delicate one, because it's about filtering out *some* of what you hear. And to do it properly, you should also use the tandem skill of Suspending, to keep an open mind.

Let's step back a moment to define why we need to Listen *through*.

As we grow up and establish ourselves as communicating adults, we develop vocal habits, tics and patterns. You could even call them signatures. They're not unusual. Just as we all lean slightly to the right or left, or as everyone's walk is ever so slightly different, the way we *talk*, the way we *sound*, develops over time. One person will develop a deeper swarthy voice. Others will emerge into adult life with a more delicate and precise way of talking. Some people have a less nasal tone than others. Some people take their inflection up at the end of a sentence. There are any number of combinations of these things, which is why no one person's voice is exactly the same as another's.

Naturally, these vocal traits become part of our character and personality and they're there to be enjoyed and celebrated. But these same habits – if they're strong or well rooted – can also do something less helpful. They can form a kind of gauze over what you're saying. A strong accent, for example, might flatten out the way you tend to Describe things. A quieter person might find it harder to emphasise something vigorously. Someone who's become used to speaking very loudly over many years will probably use less variety in their voice when they're presenting or demonstrating something.

So, as we sit there, Listening *for* information, we could easily find enough evidence for us to think:

> **"Everything about the way he's delivering this makes me wonder if it's going to happen."**

> **"The way he's talking is worrying me. It feels like he might be incredibly nervous."**

Or:

> **"My goodness, she sounds confident. She must be excited about this piece of work."**

You can see there's a potential risk to interpret people's vocal signatures – their long-term personality traits, if you like, that are deeply embedded in their way of being – as a specific clue to pay attention to. But like a good detective, you need to Listen *through* these longer-term tendencies and focus in on what the more useful, local and vocal clues might be.

The trick here? Be aware and keep Listening. As you get used to the sound of someone's voice, their rhythms, their cadences, you'll soon find your ear training itself to distinguish between an intensely boisterous man and a passionately held belief. And you'll get better at Listening *through* hearing knowing that, just because your colleague is a mildly spoken graduate, doesn't mean she doesn't have a fire in her belly and some radical ideas.

Listening *from*

When we are working with and talking to someone from another culture, it's easy to recognise the need to respect that someone might have a different perspective. So we Listen knowing that; we Check our understanding of what we hear and how they look at things. But when we are talking to people from our own culture – or someone from a nearby culture – we assume they will think like us.

Yet often their mindset – their framework – is totally different. We stop Listening for differences and assume similarities. But we're all subjective. We can only perceive the world through our own experience of it. And the truth is, we all start from different places. We have different filters; different gauzes that make us see the world through our own lens.

So, part of being a great Listener is acknowledging that those differences are present and real. And useful. Fascinating, even. And certainly eye-opening. Let me share a personal example of what can happen if you accept that we are all, indeed, different. And that you can Listen honestly, only if you allow that difference to give you space.

I first learnt to Listen *from* in a project called "Your Thoughts With Mine". Over a course of three months or so, I worked with a series of Muslim groups from around the UK and discovered that in order just to understand someone whose faith wasn't a set of religious rules or guidelines, but truly a heartfelt way of life, I needed to acknowledge that I was sitting in a completely different place to a man who, to all intents and purposes, was very like me. A father like me. A football fan like me. A middle-class mid-forties man, like me. My instinct was to find our common ground. And that took us so far.

But after a while, after we'd reached a kind of impasse in the conversation, we changed tack and decided to explore the differences between us. And they were profound. I felt embarrassed at first to admit it, but eventually I found the humility to accept that my "school of life" was less rigorous, less whole, less integrated than his. And, by acknowledging that, in fact by seeking out the distinctive differences between my perspective and his, far from limiting my capacity to Listen, I discovered I was actually freeing myself to become a deeper, more honest partner in conversation. I was free of political correctness, of caution and constraint. Instead, by openly celebrating the fact that I was Listening *from* my experience and not his, we created a defined space between us, in which we both found the oxygen to inhale, as it were. We began... to breathe. And talk. Really talk. It became a livelier, far more robust and healthy exchange. We were aware of the gap between us. And we enjoyed it. We Listened and cocreated from opposite banks of a river, because we didn't have to pretend any more that we were on the same side. We were Listening authentically, *from* our own positions. We learnt more. We laughed more. We Listened more.

So – if you're working with someone who is different to you, older, younger, more or less experienced, an expert in maths or physics, a hardened battler through trade union negotiations – it doesn't matter what the difference is. Be bold enough to acknowledge it. And you'll find yourself better positioned than ever, to Listen and learn well.

Listening *with*

Empathy is a phenomenally powerful tool. If we can't see the world at least in part, through the eyes of others, then the only life we can imagine (not just experience) is our own. And to truly Listen, to authentically Listen *with* is to empathise. And to imagine what it's like to hear and perceive the world differently. With their likes and dislikes, their perspectives and prejudices. To come as close as we can to sitting beside someone different to us and Listen *with* them through their window on the world. This is a place from which we can learn. This is a place from which we can grow. If we can Listen *with* others, we can mature and develop a richer view of their world and ours. We can begin to Listen *with* consumers in far-flung places. With customers whose lives are very different to ours. With colleagues who sit close to us, but who may be very different to us. We can all learn by understanding what it's like to be someone other than ourselves.

And we can all learn to Listen.

Key thoughts

1. To Listen well, consciously pay attention to how you tune in in order to Listen well. Clear your mind of distractions. And make sure you can see and hear whoever you're Listening to.

2. Listen *to* without distractions. Listen *for* with an open-mind. Listen *through* by making sure you don't prejudice your Listening *just* because of the way someone sounds. Listen *from* by acknowledging difference. And Listen *with to* empathise with people who see the world differently to you.

3. Finally, like a detective, Listen for the small things: the little Pauses, the clues. The things you might not be expecting. Listen for visual clues as well as verbal ones and, crucially, Listen for *how* something's being said, not just what's being said.

Listen well

One of my favourite stories is told by Chad Varah, the founder of The Samaritans, professional Listeners who provide a helpline for desperate people. He tells of a woman who came in one evening. She talked and talked and talked. Finally, after two hours, she Paused. He said: "I hesitated, then took my chance and said nothing." The woman stood up and said: "Thank you. That's one of the best conversations I have ever had."

You don't need to say anything to have a good conversation. But you do have to dedicate yourself to the role of being a Listener.

Chapter 3
Describing

Points well made and mysteries explained

Navigating

Building

Listening

Disclosing

Describing

Suspending

Checking

Pausing

Probing

Balancing

Sometimes, just a few words can create a real turning point in a conversation.

You'll have experienced this at some point, I'm sure. There's sometimes a moment in a conversation when someone's perspective is altered for ever because they understand for the *first* time what it is the other person's been trying to say. And these penny-dropping moments are created by someone being able to crystallise an idea or a thought into just a few words that seem to cut through everything else.

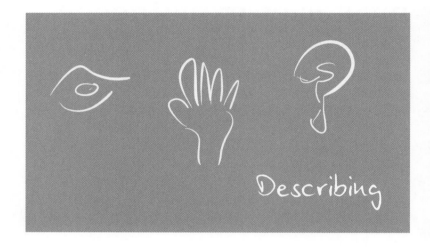

And what that person's done is to Describe something well.

(Get a cup of tea or coffee. This is a big chapter. Because really, it's about how we talk.)

Sometimes it'll be the choice of words that makes the difference to the quality of the Description. Sometimes, it's the way those words are *spoken* that carves through so keenly. In either case, it's our ability to illuminate, in just a few words, how we feel and what we mean that makes things clear and vivid for someone.

These can be dramatic moments. Moments of confession or enlightenment. Of realisation and revelation. Like the moment when you admit to your business partner:

"I think we're chasing the wrong kind of success. This isn't about money any more. It's about survival."

Or when she declares to you:

"I need to find a way to start enjoying my job again. I'm not going to quit. I want to make this work. With you."

These are *big* moments; game-changing moments in a conversation that counts. When a small act of dedicated Description cracks into the hearts and minds of the Listener. And shift happens as a result.

But great Describing isn't *always* about such a sharply focused, dramatically intense moment. Sometimes, it's more about the wide-angle lens than the close-up. And, just by paying some heightened attention to the *quality* of what we say and the way we say it, we can shift the level of expression, not just for a few seconds, but for a whole conversation.

So, whether it's in a singular axis-like moment or over a longer period of time, Describing things well can make a huge difference.

But what is it that we're actually *doing* to make this happen?

And what difference does it make?

What is it that we can change when the stakes are high?

What *are* those things we do when we Describe well?

And, most importantly, how can we do them *more*?

Let's explore this in five sections. The first four are quick and punchy. Then we'll go into a little more depth in just one area called Different Strokes in which we'll focus on understanding that *our* way of Describing isn't always everyone else's.

Take me there

Seeing someone else's point of view on a situation is a crucial part of any conversation that matters more than most. Why? Because one of the main barriers to overcome in a high stakes conversation is that of understanding difference.

Difference comes in all shapes and sizes. There are obvious examples, like a man trying to see things from a woman's point of view or an adult trying to imagine what it's like to see things through the eyes of a teenager. And then there are the more subtle differences that have more to do with an experience as opposed to the more defined differences of age or sex.

If you've travelled extensively, for example, trying to explain to someone who's never been abroad what it's like to be away from home for months at a time is going to be hard. Describing something like the intense heat of an African desert to someone who's only lived in northern Europe is going to be a struggle. And trying to get someone to understand what it's like to be immersed in the dizzying sounds of an Indian wedding is tough if your audience is a Texan without a passport. The internet's an amazing thing, but watching a video of a Delhi wedding on a computer screen still isn't much like the experience of *being* at one. So, it's not much good really, trying to Describe something to someone who has no direct reference to what you're talking about.

Except, of course, it happens all the time.

At work and in the rest of our lives, we often find ourselves needing to share experiences that others haven't had for themselves. Whether it's Describing a meeting with new partners in Shanghai or a consumer research trip to a store in rural England, when we're asked to share an experience, *how* we do it can make all the difference to our Listener getting some sense of having been "taken there".

And of course, the more unique or unusual the experience has been, the more you'll want to try and share it with colleagues. But it's hard. You've probably found yourself sometimes admitting defeat even before you've begun. The English language is littered with phrases to help us confess to our shortcomings:

"I can't even begin to tell you how busy it's been."

"I'm under an incredible pressure. You have no idea."

"It's hard to say what I mean. I honestly don't know how to put it into words."

But there *are* ways to Describe things well. You just have to be willing to focus on a few key skills.

1. For example

There's one foolproof way of being specific when you're Describing. It's the handiest short cut to being concise and it involves two magic words: *for example*.

Examples are evidence not conjecture. They have integrity. We trust them. They're the idea in action. They go behind the scenes of the general point. They're a mini-story. A case study. They're specific. They're proof that your headline has substance. That your idea's true not just in theory but also in practice. They're dependable. Which is why – in this uncertain world – we love them. So, if you find yourself making a general point and it's not being heard or, worse still, you're about to launch into a cliché, pull the emergency cord in your brain. Stop. Think. And say this sentence:

> **"Let me give you an example of what I mean..."**

Even if you don't have one to hand, believe me, once you've created that invitation to yourself to tell a story, you'll find one!

A quick tip for you. Enjoy being specific. Especially when Describing people.

You can spend a long time talking about how kind someone *is*. But it's when you tell me something specific about what that person *does* that I'll begin to understand. Give me a *for instance* and I'll have a vivid and imaginable activity to work with:

> **"For instance. Every Christmas, every year, he gets up at 4 am and gives up a whole day with his family to go down to St Martin's Lane and work in the soup kitchen."**

Now, I can start to build my *own* picture of who this man is through what he *does*.

2. Say it again

Another simple way to almost force yourself into Describing things well is to make the most of the opportunity that presents itself when – ironically – you run out of words.

Sometimes, when you're stuck for what to say next, it's because you've already said the best thing you could possibly say. You just don't *know* it yet.

So, actually, you don't have to invent more words or learn new ones. Repeating a phrase, simply *repeating* a phrase, gives you the chance to lean into what you're Describing or saying. So try allowing yourself to say the same words again, but this time with the knowledge that they *are* the best ones. The same words you lightly brushed upon just now might well be precisely the ones you need.

But this time, add a little bit of air around your words. Take your time. Add a little more weight here. A little less emphasis there. And keep it simple. You might be surprised by how good you've already been:

> **"It was a brilliant speech. It was as if everyone had stopped breathing for a moment.**
>
> **The moments after he spoke were really powerful.**
>
> ***Really* powerful."**

Just a silence, followed by the same words repeated, if they're said quietly maybe, or really slowly, will cut through like nothing else.

3. Less is more

Two words: short sentences.

That's it. Get rid of some words. Condense them. Tighten up. Be tough. Be rigorous. Be brief.

This takes longer to prepare, by the way. My experience is that the longer someone rattles on, the less thinking they've done beforehand.

And, if you want a slightly more sophisticated approach, Balance short sentences with longer ones. Enjoy trading off a short phrase or thought with an extended one.

Let me show you what I mean. Compare these two ways of saying the same thing:

> **"I think it would be a good use of time to try and create a thought-through plan that helps everyone in the organisation get their heads around exactly what it is we're trying to do. So, let's put a few ideas forward and try to come up with something that will appeal to lots of different sorts of people."**

Okay.

Now try this:

> **"It seems to me like we need a plan. A well-made plan. Not just a hastily cobbled together bunch of ideas. Rather, something that's effective, considered and thorough. Something that will capture hearts and minds. Hearts. And Minds."**

The first one is okay. But it's missing something. And that something is rhythm. It's just a long blur of words that run into each other. Whereas, in the second example, some thought has gone into how the words combine and play off each other a bit. And the lengths of the sentences are nicely varied.

So, enjoy making your thoughts – and your sentences – stand out from the crowd.

Shape it. Trim it. Extend it. And break it up. From time. To time.

4. Up the ante

Here's a very simple, but hugely impactful, way of Describing things better. Look at the words you use. Especially the verbs you use. And simply up the ante on them. Make them more specific. And work your choices a bit harder.

Don't say:	Do say:
We *did* exceptionally well last year.	We *transformed* our performance in 12 months.
I *looked* at the numbers very carefully.	I *crunched* every bit of data I could lay my hands on.
Let's *ask* ourselves what happened in June.	Let's *interrogate* what happened three months ago.
You can *take* much more responsibility.	*Flex* those muscles of yours. Much, much more.
Why not *make* it more interesting?	Compel me. Inspire me. Excite me.

5. Different strokes

There is a golden key to Describing things well. And it's to do with the ways in which we instinctively give and receive information.

There are three main channels or pathways of communication:

- visual

- audio

- kinaesthetic.

Stuff we see. Stuff we hear. And stuff we feel.

A highly *visual* person will respond to colours, brightness and any pictorial Description. They'll have an acute sense of proportion. They'll notice shapes, relative sizes and contrast more than the average person. In a conversation, they'll perceive the slightest of changes in someone's complexion, the hint of a smile or the beginning of a teary eye much sooner than other people. They're the kind of people who'll notice how ugly the air-conditioning unit is in a room.

Someone with a propensity for things *audio* will obviously be sensitive to how things sound. Not just the volume of things, but the tone of them, the variety of pitch and the complexity of what's going on in their aural environment. In conversational terms they'll detect tiny things like a slight Pause before a certain word, the faint trace of an accent or a tiny break in someone's voice. They're the people who'll notice the air-conditioning because of the noise it makes.

And the *kinaesthetic* people in the world will be touched more keenly by how the world feels physically. Anything that's connected to temperature, weight, movement and even texture is their intuitive domain. So, in a conversation, they'll use their hands more than most, they'll pick up on shifts in the way someone's sitting or leaning. And they're acutely sensitive to anything physical: the touch of a hand, a growing tension in someone's shoulders, an adjustment in posture. They're the kind of people who'll notice the breeze coming through the window. Or from the air-conditioning unit.

So, let's see if you can spot your *own* type! If you were contemplating a move into a new house, what would you notice or pay particular attention to in, say, the bathroom? Would you spot how shiny the taps are? Might you be sensitive to the amount of echo there is in the room? Or maybe you'd the flush the loo?

The truth is that we're all a mix of the three. But most of us have a strong preference as a primary channel, usually either visual or kinaesthetic. (Audio sensitivity as a lead is a rare thing, no one really knows why.) Some of us have a more pronounced preference than others, of course. But, in my experience, people tend to have one that's really strong, a secondary and obviously less strong one, and a third that's usually very low indeed. Like this:

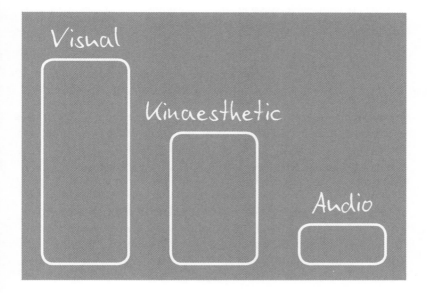

So what use is this knowledge when it comes to Describing something effectively in a conversation that really counts? Well, for a start, it might explain why sometimes it feels like you've told someone something *hundreds* of times and they *still* don't understand! The thing is, you probably *have* told them lots of times, just not in a way that they'll hear, or see or get, because *your* natural preferred channel of Description doesn't match theirs.

So, how can you tell what someone's preference is, quickly enough to be able to respond? Put simply: language. Or to be more specific: verbs. (What at primary school we used to call the doing words.) It sounds absurdly simplistic, but it's true: you can tell what type of channel someone prefers by the words they choose to use.

A *visual* person will talk about *believing* it when they see it. They'll tell you they *watch* the news, rather than picking it up it or Listening to it. When something goes wrong, they'll say things don't *look* good. And when they finally understand what's happened they'll say... (you guessed it): I see!

An *audio* person will let anyone know they approve of an idea by saying it *sounds* good. They'll consider an effective advert one that people are *talking* about in the office the next day. Ideas will *resonate* with them. If something makes sense it'll *chime* with them or at least *strike a chord*! And their way of chastising someone who's dominating a conversation will be to say they're *drowning out* everyone else. *Ring* any bells?

A *kinaesthetic* person, on the other hand, will urge progress by saying let's *move* things on now. They'll insist on *digging* out the real problem. They'll say it's time to *grasp* the nettle. They'll ask us to *seize* the day. A bad day will be one where they *wobble*. But on a good one, they'll *steam* back, *buzzing* with ideas. *Get* it?

The language you use will, almost entirely subconsciously, reflect your preference. If you're a visual person, when you're giving directions you'll instinctively talk about things that people will *see* along the route. Your instinct will be to refer to visual landmarks, like the tall stone church on the corner, the brightly lit yellow garage you pass on the right, the wide junction with stumpy trees on the left and, opposite, the glass factory with the curved roof. This is how you'll guide someone on their way, if you're a visual person. And you'll probably want to draw a map for them. And, if they get lost, of course, you'll suggest looking it up on their sat-nav.

But, if the person you're instructing is highly kinaesthetic or audio, you won't have helped them as much as you think. The kinaesthetic person wants to know different kinds of things. Is it going up or down hill? Is the left turn into a busy street – with lots of movement where the traffic is two-way – or a quiet one-way street? If you can't actually *do* the journey with them first, they'd prefer that you draw it for them on a piece of paper with them watching. Not because of the beautiful-looking map you'll create, but because of the *activity* of drawing itself. They'll watch you move the pen and translate your actions on the piece of paper into their driving instructions!

And the audio person? They're just left wishing you'd *told* them the instructions in as much detail as you've drawn them. They'll turn on their sat-nav and get their instructions from the lady with the nice voice.

So – in short, you'll find yourself able to Describe things in a conversation much more effectively if you can *tune in* to the person you're talking to. If you have a good sense of what their preferred channel is, then using the kinds of words that will do it for *them* will have a big impact. Especially if you can Listen for the verbs – because they're where the *action* is. You'll *hit* home, *get* heard or have your point of view *seen* so much more clearly and quickly if you just pay attention to their natural preferences.

When is this useful? Well, it's especially pertinent when you're trying to Describe something that's new or foreign to whoever it is you're having a conversation with.

Let's look at something that's sadly becoming more and more prevalent at work: stress and anxiety. One of the challenges that face increasing numbers of people at work is to Describe what it's like to be depressed, especially if you're talking to someone who's never experienced it themselves. If you're feeling low, this kind of Description will help a visual person see your world:

> **"It's a kind of greyness. I look at my desk and just see grey. The café. The walk to work. Even that picture there on the wall. They're all just a dull grey to me."**

If you're talking to highly kinaesthetic person, this is the kind of language that will really *carry* through to them:

> **"I feel heavy in my limbs. It's like my feet are literally leaden."**

Or, if they're audio, they're more likely to *hear* you if you Describe it like this:

> **"It's like everything's muffled. The phone ringing, people's voices, the coffee machine even, a baby's cry, music, the bell on the lift...**

they all sound like they're coming from inside a big box of blankets when I'm feeling like this."

Just a bit of extra effort on your part to Describe things in such a way that it'll be heard and understood more quickly, more comprehensively, will mean you're much better placed to have a conversation that *gets* somewhere.

So – that's a quick dip into the world of visual, audio and kinaesthetic communication styles. What are you going to do with it? Here are some suggestions:

- Establish what you think your preferred language is. (Your instinct is probably right. But test it.)

- Listen out for what language other people use. (Eavesdrop on the train or at the bus stop for practice.)

- When you next need to Describe something to someone, endeavour to speak in *their* language, not just yours.

Give it a try. You'll be surprised by how making just a few small adjustments in the language you use will make a big difference.

Key thoughts

1. A brilliant piece of Description can transform a conversation from the mundane to the magnificent. The more energy and imagination you invest in the way you talk, the more likely you are to create a turning point for those who are Listening.

2. Examples, repetition, short sentences and vivid language will make *your* story a more compelling one.

3. Understand and employ the differences in communication style between us. Use a mixture of kinaesthetic, visual and audio language to get your message across.

No words required

Describing well enables us to express ourselves. It means we can *teach* what we know and *pass on* what we've experienced and learnt. We're better able to share the insights and perspectives we have, which will increase our value hugely to those with whom we work. We can help, educate, warn, motivate and encourage people around us so much more quickly and thoroughly by giving great Descriptions. But Describing well isn't *always* about the words we use.

I once asked an Italian waitress to take part in a workshop exercise on how to Describe things well. She refused. Point blank. She wasn't able to take part, she said. "I no have words in English," she said. "I no do good in this." And I understood her reluctance. To be honest, her mastery of the English language wasn't great. But you don't need to be Stephen Fry to be eloquent. I persisted. And asked her to Describe something she loved. Something she pined for and missed from her home in Naples. "That's easy," she said. "The olive oil of my Mother," she said. "It taste so good. I cannot tell. I have no words." I asked her to try. To tell us more. I reassured her that it didn't matter how good or bad her Description was. I just wanted her to try. "Imagine you're there now. What's it like..." I asked, "when you taste it?" She closed her eyes. And went very quiet for a few seconds. And, finally, she said: "You put it on your tongue and..." She Paused. And then – I'll never forget it – this gentle, rich sound poured out of her mouth. It was a kind of sigh. A gently voiced exhalation of breath lasting only two, maybe three seconds. A sound that made *everyone* who heard it just melt. Every single man and woman in the room was captured. By her Description. And in that moment, I swear we all could have told you we'd just tasted some of that olive oil. No words were required. The Description was beautiful. And complete. Because she'd made the effort to take us there.

Chapter 4
Checking

The modest key to a golden door

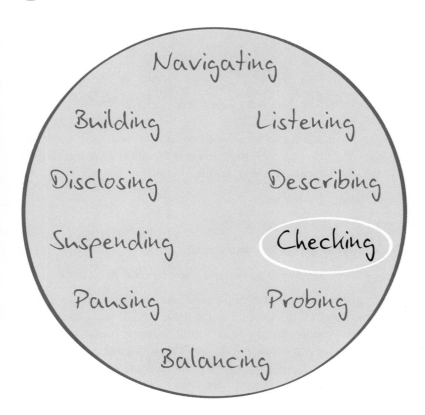

Navigating

Building

Listening

Disclosing

Describing

Suspending

Checking

Pausing

Probing

Balancing

Some skills are harder than others. And Checking is one of the simpler ones. But don't be fooled. Just a small investment in Checking creates a huge return.

So even if it takes just a little breaking-in of a new habit to Check regularly and often, let me assure you that the effort to outcome ratio with this skill is massively in your favour.

Check and you'll save time.

Check and you'll learn more quickly.

Check and you'll get briefed more accurately.

Check and you'll *know* you understand your consumer or customer.

You'll make better decisions. You'll create longer-lasting, more robust solutions to any problems you need to solve. And, if you Check, you'll find it does wonders for the relationship between you and whoever you're having the conversation with. Why? Because you'll be giving them that most precious and unique feeling that every human being wants: they'll feel understood. *Properly* understood.

So, how do you do it then? If it's so powerful a tool to have in your hands, it must be very sophisticated and complex, mustn't it?

No.

It's incredibly simple. It's just about Checking that you've really understood what someone's said to you. You need to resist the temptation to jump in with your point of view and first make sure you've taken in theirs. And the way to do that is just by playing back to your partner in conversation *your* version of what you think they meant. Not what they *said*. What they *meant*.

Checking *isn't* just repeating the words the other person has said. A machine can do that. No. You need to put *new* words to their meaning. That way, you're showing not just that you've heard, but that you've *Listened*.

So, what do you say to make it happen? The words aren't hard to imagine, but here are a few examples:

> **"Right, so what you're saying is..."**

> **"Let me just Check I've got this right..."**

> **"Okay, so for you the most important thing is..."**

Or:

> **"So, in other words..."**

Not hard, is it? And it's something we do naturally when we think it's important. Like when someone offers instructions on exactly where and where *not* to park in order to avoid a fine of £120! It's not hard to Check we've understood *them*, is it?

The trick is to make your conversation *worthy* of this kind of Checking.

(It sounds simple, because it is simple. It's up to you to change how important a conversation is.)

Time and treasure

Now you might be wondering, is this really necessary? "I think I usually know pretty much what someone means," you're thinking. "I could just end up wasting time a whole lot of time, Checking I understand *everything* someone says..."

A couple of things.

First, I have news for you: misunderstanding is the norm.

Most of the time we misunderstand (albeit slightly) what someone means. If we lived in a perfect world where everyone who talked was clear and articulate and everyone who Listened was totally tuned-in *all* of the time, maybe things would be different. But we don't. And they don't. We *all* get everything just a little bit wrong, most of the time. Which, at any one moment may not be the end of the world. But, cumulatively, it begins to matter.

And when you're having a conversation where you really need to solve a problem, it begins to matter a lot. Because the stakes are high. And if you don't Check as you go, it doesn't take long for a series of small, but subtle misunderstandings to become one hell of a showstopper. Every chasm, after all, starts as a crack in the floor. So get used to getting in there *early*.

Check quickly, lightly and often. You'll *save* time, not waste it. In a conversation where people Check deftly but continuously, it's unusual to need to have any part of that conversation *again*...

Secondly, if you're not Checking, you're missing out. Big time.

Why? Because Checking is about a great deal more than efficiency and clarity. It's also about unearthing richer, deeper content. The hidden treasures of a conversation, if you like. Because when you Check your understanding, you're not just helping yourself to understand, you're helping the person who's talking to fully *realise* what they mean.

Here's an example. You do a simple Check first...

> **"So what you're saying is that you need to find a way to start enjoying your job again? To rediscover that sense of satisfaction you had in what you do?"**

Your partner agrees:

> **"Yes, I suppose that's right..."**

But then *because* you Checked, realises *in the moment* there's something new in what you've said:

> "But actually, hearing you say it, I wonder if I've *ever* really felt *satisfied*? I enjoy my job. I just don't ever really feel satisfied. I'm always looking on to the next thing..."

Here's another example where, even though the subject's a bit tricky, you can help each other get to the heart of the issue:

> "So, what seems to be really clear, Listening to what you're saying, is that you want me to be more flexible, right? Work longer hours? Work later some nights? Come in earlier some mornings? Is that it?"

But actually, you've got it wrong. Which doesn't matter. Because the fact that you've Checked explicitly gives *them* the chance to come back and adjust your perspective:

> "No. No. Honestly, it's nothing to do with the hours. Or the time of day you do them. It's much more about the way you work when you're here. Honestly, I just need you to be more focused. And to be seen to be more focused."

So, even if, when you Check and you *don't* get a hole in one, it doesn't matter. In fact, it's a good thing. Because the person you're Checking with gets a chance to put you right and then expand their point.

Key thoughts

1. Resist the temptation to jump in with your opinion and instead first Check you understand. It keeps you in close contact with what the other person *means*.

2. Do it little and often. Make it a habit. The rewards will become clear.

3. Do it for them, not just for you. Focus on improving *your* understanding. But know that by doing so, your partner in conversation will become clearer on what they mean.

Just do it

Checking gets you to the real deal. It stops you drifting apart. It's the simple, unprepossessing key to the door of better, richer information. It's a distinct, simple skill, that'll reap huge rewards. It's the habit of all the professionally skilled helpers I've worked with: therapists, negotiators, great teachers and brilliant doctors. But it's a great habit to have. And it's easy to do. So, as they say: just do it.

Chapter 5
Probing

The art of digging deeper

Navigating

Building

Listening

Disclosing

Describing

Suspending

Checking

Pausing

Probing

Balancing

If the skill of Checking is about exploring what's already been said, then Probing is about what hasn't been said yet. When you Probe, you get beneath the surface. You dig deeper. And you find out more.

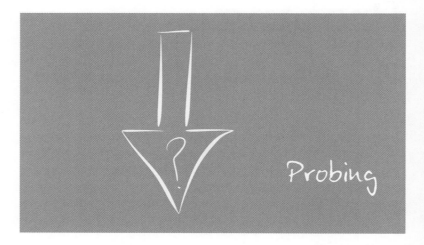

The quality of a conversation can be assessed by the extent of what it reveals. If a conversation is powerful, purposeful and productive, then one of the reasons is because you've gone beyond the *what* and into the *why*.

Probing, at its best, is a fine tool. And it's the one to reach for when you want to unearth the truth, no matter how mysterious, ugly or uncomfortable. Probe and you'll see more than content, you'll discover depth, cause and context too.

But Probing is a sharp tool. And one that warrants a certain amount of caution and care in your hands. So here are some quick guidelines on how to handle this new shiny tool before we get into some good old-fashioned techniques:

- Be economic
- Be precise
- Be patient
- Be kind.

Be kind? Yes. Attitude is crucial when you're Probing, as we'll discover here. With a tool this sharp, if you're clinical in the way you use it, you could easily and inadvertently cause or provoke a defensive reaction.

So. Warnings over. Now let's enjoy using this skill and I use the word enjoy advisedly. Probing is a fabulously enjoyable thing to do in a conversation. If you're remotely curious, this skill will probably come naturally to you. But, if you're *not* an instinctive questioner, then pay careful attention to developing your capacity to Probe. Learn it consciously as a skill and as your Probing skills improve, you may well find that it becomes second nature.

So people say if you're looking to solve a problem, if you want to get to the heart of the issue, if you want to get to where the action is, where the nitty gritty lurks and where the real answers lie... you can be sure it's time to Probe.

And here's how to do it:

1. Great questions

Probing is all about asking great questions. Closed questions and open questions. You can think of yourself almost as a boxer, with your left hand and right hand working together. Closed questions jabbing in from the left. Open questions coming in from the right.

Let's be sure we understand the difference between closed questions – which are great at encouraging short, specific responses – and open questions – which encourage a deeper, wider, more imaginative and speculative answer. Both types of question are incredibly useful – and they're best used in combination – but if you want to Probe effectively, it's vital to be aware of which one you're using when.

Closed questions

The mistake that's made often when you ask someone to define a closed question is that they're questions that can be answered only with a "Yes" or a "No". This is correct only partially. Closed questions are far more interesting than that. The most economic way to illustrate what I mean is to offer you some examples:

First there are the yes or no questions:

"Are you a sports fan?"

"Have you done this kind of role before?"

"Have you checked the numbers this week?"

Then there are other questions where yes or no won't do it, but another singular answer will:

"What do you prefer? PC or Mac?"

"Marmite. Love it or hate it?"

"Which hand do you write with?"

"So who *did* check the numbers this week? Tom or Ali?"

The answer to the last question might not be what you *expect*, but you'll still get to a single answer:

"Neither of them I'm afraid. I'll do it tomorrow."

We can start to increase the range of answers, but *still* it's a closed question:

"So where were you born?"

There can only be a singular answers to this question, but of course it could be anywhere in the world.

"When's your birthday?"

There's only one answer to this question out of a range of 365!

"Where have you most enjoyed working in the world?"

Again, there's only one answer to this, but from an even wider range.

"How many brothers and sisters do you have?"

It's a personal question but one that can only bring a definitive response.

If a particular time is involved, it'll definitely be a closed question:

"By what time *will* you have looked at the numbers?"

Again, you might not always get exactly what you're expecting, but a closed question can cover a huge range of possible answers.

"Which football team do you support?"

It might be a local team; it might be Man Utd. But it's still one team. Actually, that's not true, is it? But even if the answer is this:

"Well, actually I support our village team whenever I can, but I'm a Man U supporter, have been since I was a kid."

...it's still a closed question that ultimately gets a definitive answer. Even though you sometimes get a bit of bonus information thrown in for free!

So, closed questions are really useful when you want to:

- Encourage a shy person to speak, perhaps especially at the beginning of a conversation.

- Drill your way down to something specific. (Like getting the numbers checked.)

- Follow a trail of information to a conclusion or an end point.

Open questions

If, on the other hand, you want to provoke a deeper, more exploratory or speculative response, then that's where more open questions come into their own. Let's start with some gentle ones and then open up the throttle:

"What kind of things do you like to do at the weekend?"

That's a pretty gentle open question, partly because it could still elicit only a fairly perfunctory answer like:

"Family time. That simple. Weekends are exclusively for time with my wife and kids."

Let's open up a bit more:

"How do you look at the whole work–life balance thing?"

That's much harder to answer in a perfunctory way. The word *how* is often useful if you want to open things up. Here's another example:

"How are you finding things here so far?"

Now we're expanding the territory. It's almost impossible to respond briefly to that. But, if all you get in response to an invitation that open is a short answer like:

"Fine. Yes, all good."

... then you know you have a clear signal that you're going to have to keep digging. (See the section on Nudging below!)

Open and closed

Remember *both* kinds of questions are good and have their role to play when it comes to Probing. And, just like the boxer and his combinations, when you put a little set together, they help each other.

Just check quickly that you can tell which of this little sequence of questions is open and which is closed:

"Are you comfortable?"

"Would you like some water?"

"What kind of conversation are you expecting, I wonder?"

"Where are you with the whole restructuring question?"

"Is it a good plan, do you think?"

"At this stage, how much of next year's budget do you think it's appropriate for us to invest overall?"

"Why's that?"

And there's the word: *Why?*, quoted for the first time in this chapter. Such a small word. But it's *the* word to use when it comes to Probing. And it's where we also have to remind ourselves of how important it is when we're digging deeper to pay attention to our *attitude* as well as our action.

2. Why? Why? Why?

"Why?" is a question that children use a lot.

Why?

Because they're naturally curious. They love learning about things that fascinate them and they're hungry for information.

Why?

Because they know that the more you learn, the more interesting life gets.

Why?

They've got evidence. The more capable they are with the spoken word, for instance, the more they're involved and included in activities that give them pleasure. Like making up jokes, playing new games and deciding what's for tea.

Why?

Because adults have instincts, too. One of which is to reward the achievements of those they love with inclusion and more opportunities to learn.

Why?

Because they know deep down that nurturing, loving and developing their own children is likely to encourage in their offspring a capacity to mature, flourish and succeed, which, in turn, (they hope) will increase the likelihood that their kids will become more adept and prone to look after their ageing parents as they become old and infirm, less able to look after themselves.

Why?

Something to do with the survival of the fittest? I'm not sure I know enough about evolutionary psychology to give you a decent answer.

Why?

Because... I don't make enough time to explore and learn about things I find fascinating. I'm a grown up.

I'll stop there, shall I?

(Forgive the pop psychology. My tongue is firmly planted in my cheek. I promise.)

But there are two good reasons for that brief excursion into one of my favourite word games: asking why seven times in a row. First – I wanted to demonstrate the exercise and say that it's worth trying out – if only playfully – when you're next troubled or confused about why things are the way they are.

Second, I wanted to make a serious point about curiosity. It's the best fuel there is to fire up a good question. And when it comes to attitude, if your *reason* for asking the question "Why?" is simply to *learn*, nine times out of ten it'll be heard that way and you'll get good answers.

Think about it. We never criticise a child for asking why, because we know that what's *behind* their question is a desire to know.

If, however, you Probe *without* curiosity, or replace it with a motivation to point the finger of blame, or expose a fault in someone's argument, then the sharpest tool in the box starts to really cut through. Sometimes that might be exactly why you need to Probe, in which case off you go; a quick combination of closed and open questions will certainly get you into investigative mood:

"So, why wasn't it finished on time?"

"And why did the work stop at that point?"

"Why wasn't head office informed?"

"Why was it kept quiet?"

"Why didn't anyone think to let me know?"

The questions are really tearing into things now, aren't they?

And, whilst they're all valid questions, we've run into the biggest challenge with Probing: it's beginning to feel more like an interrogation than a conversation. Probing can tip into this space easily, where it feels too challenging, too personal or confrontational. And yet, of course, that's often why we need to Probe in a conversation that counts: because something that's been unspoken needs to be aired and confronted.

Which is why the *intention* and *attitude* behind your questions is crucial. Here are some quick guidelines for keeping your Probing both sharp and pointy and, at the same time, respectful and purposeful. You'll find that a bit of Disclosing and Navigating come in handy here, too:

1. Acknowledge the risk that a question might be interpreted awkwardly:

> **"What I'm about to ask might sound blunt..."**

> **"This could easily feel like an accusation..."**

> **"I'm conscious this is a bit of a brutal question..."**

These are all examples of Navigating: temporarily stepping out of the conversation to notice something about it in order to move things on in the right direction.

2. Then give the *real* reason why you need to ask the question. Share your intention. Your reason for asking:

> **"What I'm about to ask might sound blunt. But all I want to do is understand..."**

You're actually Disclosing here in order to Probe.

> **"This could easily feel like an accusation. But it's not. It's a real question that I think will help us get to the bottom of this."**

(Again you're using a little light Navigating to help you Probe.)

> **"I'm conscious this is a bit of a brutal question. So feel free to change it to a better one..."**

(You've Disclosed nicely here by saying what you're "conscious of" and you've Navigated gently, to include them in the direction of the conversation and you've invited their input. You're keeping the conversation safe and collective.)

3. Now you're safe to Probe freely and directly:

> **"What I'm about to ask might sound blunt. But all I want to do is understand... How and why did we lose so much money on something that's so cheap to produce?"**

(That's a nice, big, open question. It's simple and powerful. No code. No disguise. No smoke and mirrors.)

"This could easily feel like an accusation. But it's not. It's a real question that I think will help us get to the bottom of this. Why didn't we see this coming? With all of your experience in things like this, what did you miss? Where was the blind spot?"

(Can you see how there's a freedom to ask some pretty serious, direct questions now, but in a safe climate? Where the shared intention of getting to the bottom of things has created permission to get into the gritty, difficult questions you face together?)

"I'm conscious this is a bit of a brutal question. So feel free to change it to a better one. If I'm really honest, the core question for me is this: why are you the right person for this job at this moment in your career? That's the way the question keeps forming in my mind."

Again, because you've prepared the ground, you're able to ask the big hairy question honestly and simply. You're able to be authentic and share with the very person you're talking about the way you're thinking about their suitability for a prospective job. It's digging deeper, *with* them. Not *at* them. And the chances are that, because you're able to be so straightforward and open with them, they'll find it easier to be direct and honest with you.

So – asking why is nearly always a great idea. But how we do it can make all the difference.

3. Nudges

And, finally, there are a few different ways to soften up a Probe, without losing any of the incisiveness you need.

First – sometimes it helps to ask a question without asking a question. It's not shying away from Probing, not at all. It's just that there are ways to find out more without making it seem like an interview or an investigation.

Here are five quick examples of some extremely short phrases that'll encourage people to give you more information. These are especially helpful when you're dealing with the kind of people who tend to tighten up when asked a direct question, or who have a habit of giving short answers, when you'd like a bit more flesh on the bone. At the heart of them all is a request to Describe, not explain.

"Tell me more."

These are the best *three* words I know that will help you Probe without asking a question.

"Go on..."

The best *two* words I know that help you Probe without asking a question.

"I'm still not absolutely clear on..."

A gentle way of saying "Why?" without using the word itself. (Some people hate being put on the spot!)

"I wonder why that might be..."

Another way of saying "Why?" without using the word itself. ("I wonder" is the golden phrase here.)

"Because...?"

An even shorter way of asking "Why?" without actually saying it.

Keep it real

Finally, a juicy, concise tip. There's one word that's incredibly helpful when it comes to Probing.

And it's the word *really*.

For some reason, just injecting that word into a sentence encourages people to answer from a deeper, more truthful place:

"Why work here? I mean, *really*, why do you work here?"

"Let's just ask this: what's *really* going on?"

"Now then, how could we look at next year's innovations *really* differently?"

It's not a magic trick. But it feels like one sometimes. It shouldn't be this simple but it is. It just works. Try it out for yourself.

Key thoughts

1. Ask great questions. Closed questions. Open questions. And then combine the two.

2. Ask why well. Acknowledge the risks. Gain permission to dig deeper. And then enjoy the freedom.

3. Nudge people into telling you more. Make phrases like "Go on" and "Tell me more" work hard for you.

My Mum...

An ordinary conversation maintains the status quo; a great conversation disrupts it. So, in the type of conversation where you *know* you have to stir things at a deeper level to get to some great ideas or find a fresh solution to an old insoluble problem, you need to *consciously* attempt to explore what's not obviously apparent. So take hold of your sharpest tool, and use it confidently and sensitively. You're going to need to be inquisitive, tenacious, brave, honest and inventive. The ask is challenging, but the rewards are – I promise you – immense. When I was young boy, every day, as I left the house for school, my Mum would shout out to me: "Ask good questions." At that age, I'm not sure I knew the difference between a good and bad question. But, over the years, I found out. Through trial and error, I discovered the reward of asking Probing questions. And when it comes to unearthing the previously unseen and revealing the unheard, my Mum's advice remains the best I've ever had.

Chapter 6
Balancing

Keeping it rich, equal and fair

Navigating

Building   Listening

Disclosing   Describing

Suspending   Checking

Pausing   Probing

Balancing

Balance in a conversation is something we rarely notice. Until it's missing. And then, we really notice it.

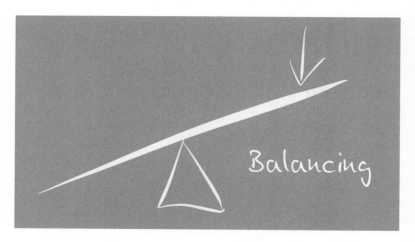

When a conversation's Balanced, it's fair, rich and productive. It breaks through the unhelpful barriers of status. No *one* person or perspective hogs the limelight. Good decisions come from considering all sides of the coin.

An *un*balanced conversation, on the other hand, is a poorer affair. It feels more like a low-grade battle than a conversation. It's frustrating, unproductive and it's prone to miss out on golden opportunities for new ideas.

In a regular everyday conversation, a lack of Balance isn't too painful or costly. Someone talks too much – so what? You don't cover all the bases? Big deal. It's a bit like having a supermarket trolley that pulls in one direction. It's annoying, but it doesn't really matter.

But, when the stakes are higher, Balance becomes crucial. If you swap your supermarket trolley for a convertible car on the motorway driving at 90 mph, you need to pay a little more attention to the state of your vehicle! So, if you have a conversation coming up that's clearly going to count for a lot, you'll want to avoid upset and escalation in a delicate or tense situation. If you want to make the best of the opportunity to solve the problems you have, you need to do whatever you can to minimise the risk involved, by paying attention to how well Balanced that conversation can be.

But, apart from avoiding disaster, what positive benefits does Balance give us in a conversation? And, in the context of a weighty conversation, what does losing Balance mean? How can we adjust things as we go, to make sure we don't get pulled off course and risk ending up somewhere we really didn't want to be?

If a conversational journey is suffering from a lack of Balance, you'll first become aware of a nagging feeling that something just isn't right. Then, if nothing is done to alter the way things are going, it'll begin to feel a much less useful way of spending your time and energy. You'll be having to work really hard to keep things on course. And, ultimately, if that annoying tilt is allowed to become a fully-fledged lean, the effect becomes more extreme and you can find yourself frustrated, annoyed, and even considering aborting your journey completely.

So how does this happen? And what can you do about it?

There are three main ways in which conversations can go wrong when they're weighted too much in one direction. Let's look at each one and identify the ways in which we can regain the Balance that will allow us to carry on the journey, rather than abandon it.

1. Taking turns

If one person's voice is too dominant, it can seriously unbalance a conversation. If you think about it, when a conversation is really hijacked by someone, it actually stops *being* a conversation at all. There may still be two people *present*, but only one is really taking part. The others stop being participants and become reluctant passengers.

So I'm afraid that, if you're the one doing the dominating, not only are you pulling control away from the other person, you're likely to be creating a pretty unhelpful tension in them too. Because the person you should be having a conversation *with* probably will have stopped Listening ages ago. Instead, all they're doing now is waiting for you to stop. So whatever response you get from them won't be anything to do with you've *said*, but a reaction to the fact that, for them, it's become a totally one-sided affair. So they're frustrated, bored and they've stopped Listening. The wheels are still turning, but the journey's happening for only one person. You.

There's a simple way to avoid this. At a very basic level, you just need to *take turns*. A huge block of one person talking, followed by another, does not a conversation make. A dialogue *isn't* a succession of monologues. You need to break down the taking turns bit into relatively short chunks. From as little as a few seconds to no more than two or three minutes at a time. No more. It may be, of course, that one of you is explaining something to the other and, ultimately, will be talking for 80 per cent of the time overall. But that one person should never talk for too long without some input from the other person, even if it's very short. They need a chance to Check they've understood, or share their surprise or throw in a quick example that Builds on a point you've made.

This takes awareness, of course. And that's one of the two key enablers you need if you want to Balance a conversation. Awareness and sensitivity are, I'm afraid, hygiene entry points for a conversation that matters. Awareness of when someone is going on for too long. And a sensitivity that allows you to break up a monologue in a way that doesn't kill its flow. If neither awareness nor sensitivity comes naturally to you – don't worry. You can still help the conversation happen. But you're going to have to start *consciously* remembering how important these qualities are and feed them in to the way you talk and Listen.

Chatty man

So, if you're someone like me, who finds it difficult to shut up sometimes, keep one ear on how long you've been talking because there are going to be times when you need to *physically* stop yourself in order to invite a short contribution from your partner in conversation. (Even when you still have stuff to say!)

So – stop, bite your lip, don't be afraid to acknowledge openly that you've been going on for ages. And hand over the baton for a while. Even if the other person's contribution is short, it's a positive thing to do. You're creating a richer, more inclusive and Balanced conversation by passing it between the two of you more often.

Now, you might be thinking: "But what if the point I'm making is a complex one? And it's going to be really frustrating to stop?" The rule still applies. You need to Disclose exactly that and say something like this:

> **"I'm conscious this is taking a little while to explain. Is it okay if I just get to the end of this particular point? Then, of course, I'll invite you in. Thanks."**

At which point people will probably say either:

> **"Yes, of course..."**

And even by them saying a few words, you've adjusted the Balance just enough for now. Or, they'll seize the opportunity you've opened up:

> **"Well, no, there's a question I need to ask now. Can you just help me be clear on whether you're talking about this year's or last year's numbers?"**

And you get a chance to clarify something that otherwise might have created confusion if you'd just carried on regardless.

So, the simple piece of advice if you're a natural talker? Don't go on for too long. Give the people who are Listening to you a fighting chance to sustain their interest and attention.

Permission to speak

What about the people who are the total opposite of chatty man? The quiet ones. The silent ones, even. Some people find it incredibly hard to speak up and participate in a conversation. But often the quietest people in the room have something to say. Just because people are reluctant to jump in at a moment's notice *doesn't* mean they don't have good ideas. But they simply need – and will wait for – an *explicit invitation* from the more vocal people to say something. It's our old friend *permission* again. It might be that you just have to be the "bigger" man or woman and help a conversation stay Balanced by openly and explicitly inviting the quieter people into it.

Here are a few phrases that will come in useful if you want to encourage a fairer distribution of talk time. Find your own words of course, but look how simply you can adjust things as you go along:

> **"I've been talking for ages. Come on, your turn."**

This is called just telling it like it is. It's simple, direct and very possible.

"Enough of my opinions for a minute. I'm interested in your point of view…"

What's particularly good about this one is that you're not just managing the time, you're actually declaring your curiosity by saying *why* you think it would be a good idea, rather than it being just efficient, or what you "should" do.

"I could go on, but I won't. Sue – what's your take on this?"

Inviting a *specific person* into the conversation can be a really good idea, first because you lose that "who's going to respond?" awkwardness. And, second, you get to open the door deliberately to a particular perspective you think might Balance things. It might be a woman's voice to offset a man's. A cynical point of view to counter a more optimistic one. An emotional response to complement a drier, more rational perspective.

Interrupt nicely

And what if you're on the other side of the fence? If you're a quieter person, more likely to end up on the sidelines of a conversation? Well, there's no escaping the fact that you need to start stepping forward a bit more. It might sound hard but, if you keep what you say *simple*, I guarantee it's easier than you think. And the difference to you and the conversation will be huge. So, take a deep breath and read on…

If you can tell that the Balance has gone in a conversation because someone really is just talking too much, you might have to interrupt them.

(Yes. Interrupting people can be a good thing to do. If you do it right.)

Interrupting can be difficult.

Because it feels rude.

But it's not rude. Not if it's done purposefully and well. And it's a lot better than signalling in that way you so easily might that you're getting bored. So *don't* slip into those horrible codes of glancing at your watch or looking at the clock on the wall. Don't sigh. Or let your gaze drift elsewhere.

In a conversation that counts, you can be better than that.

If it feels like you need to interrupt someone, the only question you need to ask is this:

Is it going to help the conversation to do it?

If it *is*, go ahead and do it. But do it like this:

First, change something in your head. In terms of *attitude*, think about it as *helping* the person you're interrupting. Because you are. You're about to help them be understood.

And in terms of the *skill*, it's not complicated.

1. Just wait for a tiny gap in their speech. A breath, a slight Pause. And, crucially, *remember what they're saying* when you stop them.

2. Then – get in there. Raise your hand a little or give some kind of signal that you're *consciously* stepping into the conversation.

3. Say that you *know* you're interrupting, but that you think you have something useful to say.

4. And then say it. (By the way, you'll find the chapters on Navigating and Disclosing helpful on this, too.)

5. Then, when you've said what you need to say, *then* you play the trump card that makes your interruption allowed. You *offer back* to the person you interrupted the words they were using *just before you stopped them*. The precise words if you can. Or as close as makes no difference:

> **"Now, when I stopped you, you were talking about the difference between profit and growth."**

Nine times out of ten (if your interruption was a useful one) they probably won't need to go back. They'll pick up from where you've taken the conversation *to*. But if they do need to go back, they can. Because you've helped them.

Believe me, interrupting someone can *save so much time* in a conversation. It's a very human thing to do. It's actually respectful if you do it for the right reasons. And, so long as you do it well and judiciously, you'll often feel *immediately* how helpful it is. And so will the people you interrupt!

Speaking up

Now, a different moment in a conversation. It's not about interrupting. In fact, quite the opposite. There's a natural moment to speak. You want to add your point of view. Someone's finished talking and you want to address the imbalance by speaking up.

But it's hard for you.

Because you're just not a very confident person. You don't have a loud voice. You're maybe not as quick as other people at expressing your point of view. So... What do you do?

Attitude wise, the tough truth is there again: you have to get over yourself a little bit. No amount of skills will help you if you can't actually open your mouth and speak. But what will help you do just that is having a few simple phrases ready. My experience is that it's very often just finding the first few words that stops shy people speaking up.

So, here are some things to say that will help you get your foot in the door.

Keeping the expectations nice and low will help you feel you can speak up. You don't have to blow everyone's minds with what you're going to say...

"Can I try something out here? I think it might be a useful addition to the conversation."

Or:

"In the interest of making sure we get a really broad perspective here, can I have a couple of minutes to put in my thoughts?"

This is a nice gentle way of carving out some space, taking the pressure off yourself to deliver it all in one brilliant sentence.

Being reflective, or shy, is sometimes perceived as a weakness. It's not. Your quietness is a strength. You've had space to absorb what's been said, in a way that the chatty people may not have had because they've been busting a gut to get in and speak. So *enjoy* being the quiet one. And reposition what Listening intently might be. People's ears might well prick up and you'll get a bit of much deserved status...

> **"I've been Listening really carefully and I think I have something useful to offer on this specific point."**

2. It's all in the mix

When you need to get to the bottom of something, when you've decided to *say it and solve it*, naturally you want the *outcome* to be as good as possible. So there's another type of Balance that will have a direct impact on the quality of what comes out of your conversations. It's not so much about time; it's about richness.

If you think about it, many of the best things in life allow for some Yin with their Yang. In a particularly delicious curry, you'll enjoy a cool yoghurt to balance the heat of the chili. Picasso's outrageous use of colour was highlighted by his delicate, sharper, hand-drawn lines. In the sporting world, the tempestuous brilliance of a flair player might steal the glory, but he can only really flourish in a team that includes hard-working, solid professionals.

Without *incorporating* difference in *some* shape or form, we risk treading a sludgy, well-worn path, rather than carving out a fresh, distinctive journey, thanks to which we see things differently.

So it's important to harvest a variety of different perspectives to give your conversation the best mix of ingredients possible. Because, without that range of different opinions, the options you're choosing and the decisions you make will be informed by a familiar run-of-the-mill exchange of similar viewpoints. Which, let's be honest, is likely to produce more of the same. Bigger, better conversations create solutions that are:

- new
- fresh
- robust
- exciting.

And bigger, better conversations need a mix of nourishing ingredients. So create a rich, Balanced mix. And your outcomes will improve hugely.

How do you do it?

Different strokes

Let's get into this by being deliberately polarised at first. We can get more subtle later.

A good conversation *embraces difference*. In fact, a really good conversation seeks it out. Because if only *one* side of the story is told, as Listeners we're not getting the whole picture. We might, for instance, be hearing only a male perspective. A female one. An old one. A young one. A rational one. Or an emotional one. They might all be perfectly valid perspectives in themselves. But they're not complete. They're not Balanced.

Let's take, for example, a conversation about being more effective in a particular working practice, it doesn't matter which one. The point is that the purpose of the conversation is to look for new ideas.

It's obvious, isn't it, that if you hear *only* the voices of people who've been around for a long time, you're more likely to have a more cynical, "been there done it" tone of voice dominating proceedings. You're unlikely to get the fresh perspective you need.

Equally, however, if the only people you talk to have joined recently, you'll get a different, but just as unhelpfully, skewed perspective. Their opinions might be fresh and uncynical, but there's a danger they could also be naive, unrealistic or simply irrelevant to the problem you face.

So both perspectives are valuable, but neither should be heard alone. And, as someone who wants to create the best conversation possible, it's your job to get that mix right. To find a Balance between them.

So ask for it. Explicitly. Navigate lightly first and then invite different points of view by saying things like:

> **"Okay. It seems to me that so far we've heard plenty of opposition based on practicality. Does anyone oppose the plan because it's not ambitious enough?"**

It's not complicated. It's just a deliberate invitation to bring in a point of view from a different and particular perspective.

"Right – I'm happy that we've got the numbers right. We're in at a bargain price compared to our rivals. But what about creatively? Who's got an informed opinion on how well we stack up against the competition in that sense?"

That's how you get rich and Balanced input. You ask for it. You invite it in. Explicitly.

Let's touch just lightly on the more subtle riches to be found here.

Even if there are only two of you in a conversation, you can get a much better mix of input by being fully aware of what resources are available to you, simply by being the richest version of the person you are and bringing all of those aspects of your personalities to bear.

We all have different strengths, weaknesses, areas of expertise, qualities and personalities to bring to the table. But often, we tend to restrict our own palette. It's almost like there's a tendency to typecast ourselves: "I'm more of a realist." "You're the creative one in this relationship." "Let's admit it: you're good at thinking things through; I'm more impulsive."

I'm the first to say that playing to your strengths is a great thing. And there are many tests and lenses on personality types that can help us understand what those strengths might be. The famous *Thinking Hats* of Edward de Bono, the Myers Briggs personality types (I was an INTP the last time I looked), the Belbin preferences (I think I'm a Plant, but I can't remember); these are just a few of the most well-known tests I can remember without even thinking too hard. There are many, many more.

So, by all means, we should bring our preferences to bear. Let optimists be optimistic! Encourage the safety-conscious to be conscious of safety. Whichever is your preferred currency for understanding the people you work with, you should draw consciously on those strengths. When you want to create a really strong mix of ideas and possibilities, you need to get the most you can out of however many people are involved in the conversation.

But, in a truly Balanced conversation, you ought to be aware not just of what you *have*, but of what you don't have. Some perspectives might be missing. And that can be costly.

- What if neither of you is an instinctive long-term thinker?

- What if no one around the table has the inclination to test something before you follow through on a hunch?

- What if no one in the team is instinctively radical or bold creatively?

So, here's where Balancing gets creative. To get the richest mix possible, it may not be enough to play to your natural strengths in a conversation. You might have to push yourself to work that imagination muscle a little bit and say things like:

> **"Let's try thinking differently about this. We're good earners. We'd buy this product on a whim. What if we were on the minimum wage?"**

Or, even, if you're trying to work out a good package for a potential job candidate:

> **"We're both pretty ambitious people. And maybe he's not like us. Maybe what we'd be tempted by wouldn't attract him as much."**

And, culturally, as our frames of reference in business expand more and more, it pays huge dividends to imagine out of our own context:

> **"It strikes me that we might be being very Western about this. If we were Muslim women in a rich district of Delhi, what would be important to us then?"**

We're getting well into the territory of the imagination here. But, sometimes, in order to create a good mix, that's exactly what you need to do. Because not all the perspectives you need are in the room.

3. The Balance of power

And now to the last element of Balance: power.

Power comes in many shapes and sizes. The best way I know to illustrate this point is the story a brilliant Lebanese peace negotiator told me about a conversation he had been having with an Israeli counterpart. "The thing is," he told his Jewish partner in dialogue, "you've got all the status in this relationship. You have the relationship with the USA, you have money and you have the nuclear weapons. So, you're going to have to seriously step down to meet us, if we're going to have anything like an equal conversation."

The Israeli negotiator came back immediately. "I agree with you," he said. "Partly."

"We have status." he said. "Of course we have status. But you know something? There's quite a lot of status involved when you stroll into a Tel Aviv café with a time-bomb strapped to your chest."

Whatever its form, a mismatch in status can unbalance a conversation easily. It might spring from a difference in age or experience, pay packets, job titles, or relative abilities to think analytically, creatively or practically. Each combination of people brings its own inequalities, some obvious, some less so. And differences in status aren't going to go away. Seniority, hierarchy, experience, age, different levels of pay. These things exist at work. So the question isn't how to ignore them or get rid of them. The question is how do we work with them?

Briefly, it's a three-step programme.

First, you need to *notice* the difference. One person will often have more status than someone else. It might even be that whoever has the higher status in terms of experience has less status in expertise. An MD in his fifties may be on better money than a 23-year-old who works in IT, but she probably knows ten times as much as the man who, technically speaking, is her boss. Whoever has the power, it's crucial to be conscious of it. Be alert to it. If you're an oldest child, then you'll probably be used to being given status. If you're a kid brother or sister, it might not be something you're so familiar with.

Second, you've detected the difference. Time to *acknowledge* it.

You've *seen* the situation. Now *state* the situation. As it is. Clearly and concisely:

"You're obviously much more informed on this than I am. Let's not pretend otherwise."

The sheer relief of getting something like this out in the open is a strong sign that an authentic conversation is happening. You're sending a clear signal out, that it is what it is. And you're okay with it.

"Look, I have first-hand experience of exactly this kind of problem from my previous job. And I don't think you've encountered this before."

Whenever this kind of imbalance is declared openly you can almost feel the air change in the room. (You're also using the skill of Disclosing here, by the way. You're saying what's on your mind. A necessary and powerful step on the path to getting somewhere.)

So, having aired and acknowledged that there's a lack of Balance, it's time for the third step: you need to *counter* it. Like adding ballast to the side of the ship that's tilting up out of the water, you can put some extra weight on the side that needs it:

"I'm happy for you to lead on this. It makes sense. But, first, just let me give you an outsider's point of view, my naive but honest perspective..."

Balance is restored. Now you're *openly* sharing the responsibility of keeping things steady. You're literally sharing the power. You're both putting your best foot forward. And putting yourself in a great position to get a good result out of the conversation. Because you're working on it together. You're both in on it. No secrets. No hidden concerns about who's better than who. No one's privately playing God and manipulating the conversation. It's a joint effort. And it'll begin to sound like that:

"If you like, I can tell you how I read what's going on. Given that I've seen such a situation like this before. But please Listen for any false notes in what I say. It's possible I might project one team's issues onto a totally different set of circumstances."

So there you go. Three steps to deal with a conversation where the Balance of power is tipping too heavily in one direction. Notice it. Acknowledge it. Counter it. Together.

Key thoughts

1. Take turns. Make sure no one (not even you) talks for too long.

2. Balance means richness. A great conversation looks at things from North, South, East and West.

3. Power comes in different shapes and sizes. An equalised conversation is a healthy one.

Practice makes perfect

I got my first moped for my 17th birthday, in the middle of winter. And I remember, at the time, being astonished that I was allowed just to get on and ride it with an automatic provisional licence. No one ever taught me the skill of keeping it upright, so I learnt the hard way. I skidded on the ice, took the odd bend too late and fell off a few times. Luckily, it had a top speed of only 30 mph and we lived in the countryside where there were lots of empty roads, so I was never badly hurt, just a bit bruised and embarrassed. By the time I was allowed on a bigger machine, I'd learnt for myself the importance of the one skill no one teaches you as a young motorcyclist: Balance. So here's a hint.

Practise the skill of Balancing in a conversation where there's little to lose. In a chat with a friend. A loose discussion on politics, fashion or football. Or a catch-up on the weekend with your colleague.

You'll learn in safe circumstances – just like I did – that on an important journey, like a high-stakes conversation, where there are risks and twists and turns, staying Balanced is more than a basic skill – it's a crucial one.

Chapter 7
Pausing
Time to think

Navigating

Building

Listening

Disclosing

Describing

Suspending

Checking

Pausing

Probing

Balancing

"Sometimes, the best thing you can say in a conversation... is nothing."

(This is my attempt at a pause in written form. You probably guessed that already.)

Pausing is such a simple thing to do in a conversation.

And it's as simple as it sounds.

It's just about stopping. For a few moments.

Nothing to it.

Except there's plenty to it. And actually, it's not *stopping*, which sounds like an ending. It's Pausing. Which is more like a beginning.

Mechanically, Pausing *is* simple. You just refrain from talking for a while. You let the noise stop and allow silence to happen. But it's not a mechanical process. And just because it's a simple idea doesn't mean it's easy to put into practice. In fact, when it comes to *actually* doing it, rather than talking about it, Pausing for many people is one of the *hardest* things to do in a conversation.

Why?

Well, for many of us it's counter-intuitive; it goes against the grain. So, for some people, it can feel *really* awkward. Which is a shame because in a Pause that you create – and it may last for only two or three seconds – *so* much can happen that *helps* a conversation go well.

- You can imagine.
- You can reflect.

- You can process.

- You can change your mind.

- You can come up with an idea.

- You can think.

Yes. You can *think*.

In some cultures, like Japan or Finland, silence isn't an unusual part of a conversation. People tend to be far more comfortable when there's a temporary lull in the words there being spoken. It's accepted as a normal part of the way in which people think and work together. So, if you happen to hail from Helsinki or Tokyo, Pausing will come much more easily to you. But, in most Western cultures, where there's a more prevalent belief that if you're not talking, we're not getting anywhere, saying nothing is a much less common occurrence. So, if you want to introduce a Pause into a conversation, you're going to have to be explicit about *why* you're doing it.

It's a rare skill, this. And there's an embarrassment factor for many people about using it. But, if and when you do, the very same people who find silence awkward are nearly always the first to be grateful that someone else has done it for them.

So let's look at how to Pause more and see if we can't make it feel a little less cumbersome when we do.

The sound of silence

What's the problem exactly? Why *does* Pausing feel like such an unnatural thing to do for so many of us?

Well, silence, or at least the absence of anyone talking, *can* feel like a waste of time. Especially when you're not sure if it's a deliberate silence or not. Just a short lapse in most conversations will provoke a stream of words coming from *someone's* mouth and even a slight Pause will create a strong instinct to get in there quickly and fill the gap. It's almost irresistible. But it's *worth* resisting. Because our thinking is better when it's got a bit of air around it. When it's allowed to breathe. When the mind is given a little bit of pure oxygen time. So, the simple truth is that you can seriously improve a conversation by *not* saying anything.

Think before you speak

Let's look first at how, by Pausing, you can create Time and Space for other people.

Here's a question for you. When is it important to think before you speak?

Always? No.

Never? No.

Sometimes? Yes. But those sometimes might be more than you think.

A quick caveat, though. There are moments in a conversation when a swift, unmonitored response is a great idea. Moments when it's a strong human instinct simply to *react*. When we're asked a direct question. When a provocative point of view comes our way. Or when someone throws into the conversation something totally unexpected. There are any number of trigger moments in a conversation that will quick-release that tightened coil in our mind and, before we even know it, we're pinging back a hair-trigger response. We speak immediately and without thinking. And sometimes it's important, interesting and appropriate just to say whatever springs to mind. But...

When the stakes are high, when there's tension, sensitivity or fragility, when a small false step might easily upset the apple cart, it's probably going to be worth biting your tongue and thinking for a moment before you speak. How many times, after an important conversation, have you said to yourself, "Damn! If *only* I'd thought first, before I opened my big mouth!" "I must stop doing that," you say. Well... yes and no.

Thinking *before* we speak is something we all want to do in hindsight. But the trick is to do it at the time. And the way to do that is to start thinking about it much more *positively*.

It's not something you need to *stop*. It's something you need to *start*.

You need to start Pausing. And here's how to do it.

Permission to Pause

In a conversation of substance, most of us, before we speak, need just a moment or two. To take in what's been said. To reflect or prepare what we want to say in response. To consider the impact of what we want to say, perhaps.

So the bluntest piece of advice here is obvious:

Take that moment.

Easier said than done? Of course. And the worry that *most* people have about doing this, is that it's going to feel clumsy. Don't worry, there's a key to the door. And it's a precision-cut key called permission.

If you can lightly give or gain *permission* for it, a Pause doesn't have to feel *anything* like as awkward as you might think.

How exactly do you create permission? What words can you use? Well, as in all these things, your own words will be the best ones, so give it some thought and you'll find your own language.

But, to get you going, here are a few easy phrases to nudge you in the right direction.

Simple words work best:

> **"Hold on for a moment. I'm just thinking. Let me… just collect my thoughts for a second."**

(Pause.)

Or:

> **"Okay – I have a few thoughts on that… Give me a moment."**

(Pause.)

You can add in saying *why* you need to Pause, too. Almost certainly you'll find this makes it feel even more natural and much less weird!

So try something like this:

> **"Just bear with me. I'd like to try to save time for all of us, by saying this simply but well…"**

(Pause.)

Good work. You've bought yourself some precious thinking time. (And, in case you're interested, you've just Disclosed and Navigated. See? You're already good at this.)

Now… you have a Pause. Use it. *Keep thinking.*

> **"So…**

(Nothing wrong with the verbal equivalent of dot, dot, dot, if it helps…)

(Pause.)

> **"Okay. I've got it. It's about loyalty."**

And you're off! You created permission for the Pause. You used the time to do some thinking. And you've come up with a succinct and distinct point of view. And all because you simply gave yourself a few seconds.

I admit it doesn't always happen *quite* so easily. But trust me, it's kind of astonishing how just a slight Pause can help you to phrase something concisely and clearly, rather than waffling on for ever. Just a few seconds of Pause can be a small investment with huge yields.

So – there you go. Pause more, to help yourself think more. And save time.

Kill a question

Now, how about helping others by Pausing yourself? Occasionally?

Let's say you're at a certain point in a conversation – maybe in an important meeting or a one-on-one – where you've been considering something for a while, and you come to a natural end with a question. Like this:

> **"So overall, I think it feels and looks like a thought-through plan. It's ambitious. Which I like. But… it also makes me nervous. What if it goes wrong?"**

Obviously, this is just an example question, but the point here isn't the content, it's the *moment* in the conversation to which I want to draw your attention. It's a moment where you've landed on something. A strong point of view that's inviting a response. Or, as in the example, a question. These moments are significant *junctions* in a conversation. They're the moments when a small idea might get developed. A deeply held belief is challenged. Or a new thought is provoked. So, potentially... it's an optimum moment for a really useful Pause; a few moments for people to think and consider the possibilities.

So... you leave a Pause, right?

You Pause.

You sit there.

In the quiet.

And wait.

For as long...

As it takes.

No, you don't.

That's *not* what we tend to do. There's a really strong natural urge to talk, isn't there? Instead of letting what we've said just *sit* there and be a big, useful thought-provoking question, how many times have *you* given in to the urge to jump in on yourself with more words?

The words we're tempted to compose come in a series of variations (all well-intentioned, of course):

- **Variation 1:** You talk in an attempt to clarify.

   "You know. I mean what if we try it and then it doesn't quite go exactly the way we expect it to..."

(The intention here to be clearer is a good one. But, actually, all you've done is repeat the same question. And put a bit of noise into what *was* a nice quiet thinking space.)

- **Variation 2:** You lose your nerve and start to dress up what you've said with conditions and caveats.

> "I mean obviously we'd be careful, and we'd do everything we can to mitigate against anything going wrong..."

(All you're doing here is retreating.)

- **Variation 3:** You might just put the sentence slightly differently, in case anyone didn't understand it the first time.

  > "What if everything we've done to make it a success... counts for nothing?"

(All you're doing here is repeating.)

- **Variation 4:** Or in the event that no one responds immediately, you're tempted to try and make it easier for everyone and make it a more manageable question.

  > "I mean... Maybe we won't hit the right numbers. Or perhaps the take-up will be too much and we'll be over-subscribed? Or the business context changes..."

Again, you're being helpful. Or *trying* to be. And, naturally, *all* of your suggested scenarios *could* be really useful provocations in one direction or another. But they're not necessary. Not yet. And by being more specific and using examples straight away, you've turned what was a nice big open question into a multiple-choice test. Or a quiz. Now there's nothing wrong with a quiz. It's just not as interesting as getting people to use their imaginations. And by not allowing a Pause to happen, you're lessening the chance of generating some rich thinking in others.

So.

After a good question...

Just...

Pause.

Don't be tempted to rescue people from the silence.

Let them sit in it.

Just for a few seconds.

Now, if the sound of silence is *too* much and you feel you *have* to speak, don't be tempted to add anything to the content. Just gently give permission for the Pause, by saying something as simple as:

"Take your time."

"Just take a minute to think about it."

Or:

"There's no rush."

Remember, a Pause gives people a chance to *think*, maybe a bit more deeply than they otherwise would have done. So, in that sense, it's a huge act of generosity. You'll be well thanked for it. If you can hold your nerve.

And, if it feels like the Pause is creating a bit of gentle pressure to come up with something interesting... that may not be a bad thing. If you've given permission for it, the Pause won't feel *too* uncomfortable. And a bit of a squeeze might be just what the conversation needs.

So have faith. Ask the question. And allow the Pause.

A response will come.

And, when it does, it'll probably be all the better for a bit of silence around it.

Key thoughts

1. Give permission for the Pause with a gentle reminder that there's no hurry.

2. Don't be tempted to add words to a well-asked question.

3. Hold. Your. Nerve.

Warning

Pausing in a conversation really isn't any more complicated than that. But even though it's simple, you might be one of the many people who'll find it one of the toughest skills to put into practice, especially if you're not used to it. For what it's worth, I honestly think that Pausing is one of the most disproportionately powerful of all conversation skills. The ratio of effort to benefit makes it massively worthwhile. And the space you create by Pausing is such a rare and valuable thing in today's hectic, frenetic world of work. I promise you, people will so value your efforts to create space in a conversation. So, even if you feel a little self-conscious when you try it for the first time, get over the potential for mild embarrassment. Create permission for Pause as your key to the door. You'll find that by gently insisting on everyone occasionally doing very little, you might be doing a great deal.

Chapter 8
Suspending

Who knows?

Navigating

Building

Listening

Disclosing

Describing

Suspending

Checking

Pausing

Probing

Balancing

Suspending (essentially) is keeping an open mind. It's the opposite of assuming. And it's about putting aside your own prejudices – if only temporarily – and considering an alternative point of view.

It's a rare thing to come across as an intuitive skill.

(And I'd happily bet good money you don't know many people who are intuitively good at it.)

Why?

Because it's in our nature to make judgements. Quick judgements. Particularly when we have little time. We jump to conclusions. We make snap decisions. There's an instantaneous impulse in us to make meaning immediately. To process, assess and judge. The digital age reflects our primal urges neatly. Thumbs up; thumbs down. Like; don't like. Clever; silly. Funny; boring. Will work: won't work. Good thing; bad thing. This intuitive ability we have to categorise and move on comes, it would seem, from deep within, ingrained as it is in our ancient crocodile brain.

And the truth is, I think that it's a blessing *and* a curse. Every time we cross the road, pour the kettle or reach to catch a falling object, we put this brilliant talent to work with positive effect. But it's a troublesome feature of humanity, too. Creativity, collaboration and communication all suffer at the hands of swift judgement. In conversation terms, perhaps the most common example of this is the apparently harmless response to a brief Description of... well anything really with:

"I know *exactly* what you mean."

To which the only honest answer can be:

"Do you? Really?"

Quick judgement is an impulse that generates its own problems. It creates overly simplistic stories out of complex narratives. It can reach towards only what's known, not what's imagined. And it puts a lid on things as early as possible, even if a more thoughtful approach might be required. In the Western world of work, quick judgements are hailed often as effective and necessary. And no doubt that's true. Sometimes. Some of *my* best decisions – like some of my best conversations – have, indeed, been quick and decisive ones. But, like you, I'm sure, some of the most important choices I've made have also benefited from conversations that entertain conjecture, that demand reflection and allow for new and emerging ideas.

And it's these conversations – the ones that *aren't* there to create immediate judgement or assessment – that could certainly benefit from a little more Suspension here and there.

So – let's look at what Suspending means in practice. And how we could do it more.

Bracketing

When something comes up in a conversation that just feels or sounds wrong, even if it's small, it can upstage everything else that's happening, including (most importantly) your ability to Listen. Let's say you're talking with the woman in charge of financing a major project. A conference, say. And let's say you're working on the basis that you have a budget of €50,000 to put on the whole thing. So, you meet with the project team and, suddenly, out of nowhere, comes a bit of a surprise from the head of finance:

"Whatever we do, we need to come in on or under budget. We
certainly can't be going over the maximum we've been given.
€20,000 is more than enough for an event like this."

Cue the alarm bells. "Did she say €20,000?" you're thinking. "€20,000?
We'll never pull this off for that little!"

And, from that instant on, whatever else is going on in your head fades
away. You're thinking constantly now about the revised sum of money.
You're reinventing ways to feed 150 people. You're looking for a new
venue. You might even start Googling for a new job, given that you've
spent half your supposed budget already.

And then, a few minutes down the line, your financial executioner comes
back to the topic of the budget and says:

"Let me make something crystal clear. I want to keep the hotel
and accommodation bills distinct from whatever it is we put on
stage. That's why we're running separate budgets and accounts.
Understood?"

Ah. The relief! There you were, including hotel costs in your budget.
You're okay. It's €20,000, *plus* hotel and accommodation costs. You can
breathe again! But wait... she's not finished:

"Any questions on anything I've said there?"

And that's when you realise that you've not heard a single word. Of
course you haven't. You've been obsessing over what you *assumed*
was true. You thought you'd made a terrible mistake. The last thing
you've been capable of doing was *Listening!* You made your superfast
assessment that something had gone wildly wrong somewhere and that
you must have been given the wrong information and assumed you were
in the deepest kind of trouble you can possibly imagine.

And now you're not.

But you've missed a whole load of useful information because you were
so busy worrying about something that turned out to be nothing. (So
much for the usefulness of the quick judgemental mind.)

I'm sure you've had similar experiences from time to time. You've missed
out on some crucial piece of information because you were distracted by

a nagging doubt about something that's just been said. And your brain can't leave it alone.

Except it can. But it needs your help. And here's how to do it.

It's called bracketing and it comes straight out of the world of psychological techniques. Essentially, when something comes up, a look, a word, a fact, a figure, that brings out that judgemental instinct, don't pretend it's not there. You know it is. So acknowledge it. But put it into brackets. *(Like this.)* Put it to one side. You can do this either literally, by writing it down and putting the piece of paper to one side, or you can just trick yourself into putting imaginary brackets around that word and then letting it float on your right-hand side. Just out of shot, as it were.

Often, you'll find you'll have judged too early or without just cause. And guess what? Your brackets dissolve. Whatever the reason, the concern you had will evaporate. It'll melt away, the brackets can disappear and you can keep Listening. But what if that *doesn't* happen? What if the brackets start to glow and stare at you? Well, *then* you bring the word, the idea or the concern you had *back* into focus. You bring what was in the background to the foreground at an appropriate time. You Disclose openly that you're having a problem with it and it gets dealt with.

It's a classic process of dialogue this. Try it. It really works.

Wonderland

Next up on the list of how to make being open-minded a practical thing to do is the notion of curiosity. This particular "c" word is the mother of invention and the sworn enemy of cynicism. If you remain curious, if you have the guts to "wonder" what might happen, you'll find yourself in the space of true creativity.

There's not much more to say about curiosity and wonder, really. Except that they're a good idea. And they're especially important when you're having a conversation where the *purpose* is to come up with new ideas.

As an example of this in action, imagine the day in the late 1980s – when people were still putting tape cassettes in Sony Walkmans – when someone first put forward the idea of a handheld device that could hold tens of thousands of songs, with no visible moving parts. There will have been a hundred different reasons why anyone could have objected to such a ludicrous suggestion. And I'm sure people will have said things like: "You know what? The Walkman is how we Listen to music on the move. We just need to work harder on making batteries last longer." But enough people stayed curious. Enough people said: "Hang on a minute. It sounds crazy. But I wonder. What if? What if we could make that happen? What then?"

And so the iPod was born.

Talkin' about a revolution

The final thing to say on Suspending is this. It's *the* skill to bring to bear when all but the last bit of hope is extinguished. When you're stuck in a corner. When nothing seems to make sense any more. It takes courage to do sometimes, but that deep inhalation of breath that precedes the radical suggestion or the asking of the "unaskable" question is often the herald to a totally new way of thinking. You release the breakthrough that solves the problem. You find the missing piece of the jigsaw or the paradigm change you've been struggling to imagine.

I know I've been involved in countless conversations where it seems like we've totally lost our way. And then someone Suspends normal service and says something like this:

"I think... I might be changing my mind."

"Maybe this isn't going to be quite what we thought it would be..."

"If we're going to change that... maybe we should change this, too."

"Wait a minute. Maybe we're right. And everything *except* this bit is wrong."

"What would happen if we reversed the order completely?"

These are the thoughts that change worlds. They're the moments in which great ideas are born. And they come only if at least one person in the conversation literally opens their mind, Suspends what they would normally think or believe... and entertains a new possibility.

List of requirements

So, to genuinely Suspend requires many things, but these are the big ones:

- generosity (or at least a sense of optimism);
- confidence;
- putting your ego to one side;
- a willingness to consider ideas and possibilities that at first might seem absolutely crazy.

Key thoughts

1. Bracket contrary or distracting thoughts. If you feel a wave of assumption breaking over you, acknowledge it. Put it in brackets and keep Listening.

2. Maintain a sense of wonder. Be curious.

3. Be prepared to change your mind.

Diversity of thinking

Carlos Ghosn, the renowned ex-CEO of Honda, talks about how people learn from diversity but are comforted by commonality. And it's worth noticing, I think, that, generally, we take comfort in life by seeking out things and people that reinforce our world view. But our world is changing. And we're having to change with it. Old habits and ways of thinking are making way for new insights in the global world of technology, health, politics, religion and, of course, working practices. So much is new. And we have to deal with difference every day. So if we *have* to learn, we might as well be curious. And that means Suspending judgement, looking beyond the obvious and into the worlds between cultures, between ideas, between people. While being between things may not always be the most comfortable position, it's where new space lies. So, try putting your ego to one side for a few moments. Listen openly to the other person, no matter how different they are to you. Suspend your judgement. You never know: you (and the conversation you're having), might be on the verge of creating an amazing new idea.

Chapter 9
Disclosing

Putting your background into the foreground

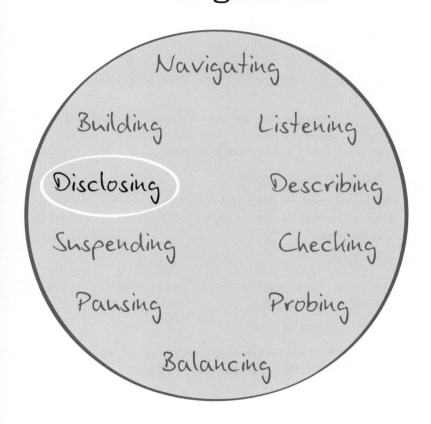

Navigating

Building

Listening

Disclosing

Describing

Suspending

Checking

Pausing

Probing

Balancing

This is one of the skills that is simple to Describe. But, more than any other, sometimes it can feel like it's really hard to do.

Essentially, Disclosing means saying what you're thinking. Which sounds like a great idea. But when you think about it, there are *many* good reasons why you might choose not to do that.

You might *upset* the other person:

> **"This isn't working, is it? I honestly don't think you have the right kind of temperament for this kind of job. I'm sorry, but we have to change things."**

It might appear *rude*:

> **"I know you want the promotion. But it's just so clear to me that you're not ready for it."**

You might appear to be *stupid*:

> **"I'm sorry, but I don't understand what you've just said. I'm sorry. I know I shouldn't be, but I'm just really confused."**

They say usually there are three voices in most conversations: the one inside your head, the one inside the other person's head and then the actual dialogue. And, of course, sometimes it's hard to say openly what you are really thinking in the conversation that's heard by everyone. But it's *not* impossible.

Preparation

The most helpful thing you can do to help you to be honest in a conversation is to give permission for it right at the beginning. So, you'll be helped hugely to put this skill into practice, if you've Navigated well at the start of your conversation. If you've both clearly put on the table the fact that this conversation counts *enough* to be honest. Maybe because it's just one of those "cards on the table moments" that happen in life. Maybe because there's been a crisis of some sort and there's no option now but to face up to the truth. Or, more positively, maybe your relationship with the person you're talking with has changed, so you can now trust each other more.

Whatever the circumstances are, if you've included them in your Navigation at the beginning, you'll have increased significantly the potential for anyone involved in the conversation to Disclose openly. Because – if you like – it was in the contract!

But still, at the precise moment when it's time to really say what you're thinking, you'll want to know if you can *actually* open up and speak your mind, if you really could and should speak freely. This is the crunch moment. The stakes are high and you're super conscious that the next move will really count. Your mind steps up a gear, searching for the question that's going to help you determine if it really is a good idea or not to be totally honest.

Question time

There are a lot of questions that you're likely to ask as you find yourself on the threshold of being honest. Some of them are terrible. Like, for instance:

"Why not just blurt this out and hope for the best?"

Answer: Well of course you *could*. But then you could also play a round of Russian roulette.

Or:

"What's the worst that could happen?"

Answer: Probably you have absolutely no idea. And now's not the time to start writing *that* list. Seriously, though, you could justify this question in lots of ways. But it's not a very positive way of looking at it.

And, if it's a senior person you're talking to and there's something you've wanted to say for a long time, there might even be a voice in your head that's asking:

> **"Even if I get sacked for saying this, how much do I want to keep this job anyway?"**

Answer: Probably more than you think. That's why you've spent all this time putting off this conversation. So don't be reckless.

But let's not ask these questions. They're not good enough.

Here are a couple of better ones:

> **"If I say what I'm thinking, is it going to help *me*?"**

Or:

> **"If I say what I'm thinking, is it going to help *them*?"**

These are especially good questions if you ask them both.

But there's a better one still. A much better one. And it's this:

> **"If I say what I'm thinking, is it going to help the conversation?"**

This is the question to ask. Because, especially if you've taken time to Navigate at the beginning, if you've decided *together* on the purpose and territory of the conversation, *this* is the question that will guide you in terms of the level of candour you can both afford safely.

Let's test the theory with a tough example. A situation when you find yourself wanting to draw your boss's attention to the fact that – as you see it – other people aren't pulling their weight.

Let's imagine you *want* to say this, or something very like it:

> **"There are people in this team who are, frankly, shirking their responsibility. On a long-term basis. And one of the reasons they're continually getting away with it is because they know, even if you find out, you won't come down hard on them."**

Tricky content, isn't it? But let's imagine that all the facts are true. So it's important. And it's not a bad example of the kind of sensitive subject that can go un-Disclosed for months, at huge cost in the shape of wasted time, frustration and resentment.

So think again about the question we asked just now:

"If I say what I'm thinking, is it going to help the conversation?"

What would be the answer to that question right now?

If your *goal* is to get to the bottom of things, then I'd say the answer is "Yes." A definite yes. But, before we make our move, let's just check in on whether asking the *other* questions would have led you to the same decision to press on.

First, is it helpful to *you* to say what you're thinking? Well – quite possibly not. It puts you in a position of personal risk. You're close to ratting on people. And no one likes a squealer. And what if you're wrong? What if, actually, you're not quite as fully furnished with the truth as you think you are? What if the shirkers are actually working on a project you know nothing about? Or what if someone you suspect of laziness is actually ill? On reflection, if *all* you ask is the question "Is it a good idea for *me*, if I say what I'm thinking?" you may well end up saying "No it's not." So you revert back to the codified language, resentment, insinuation and semi-suggested hints. Welcome back to the dark world of half-spoken truths. (The very place from which you were trying to escape.)

Now, let's take the other pretty good, but not good enough, question: is it a helpful thing for your boss to hear you speak your thoughts out loud? Again – it may well not be. What might happen? They'll be landed with an unexpected jab to the ego because they'll probably hear little else other than the fact that they're being taken for a fool. (And no one likes that.) And no boss is so on top of things that they can filter out totally the personal criticism that's laced into this sort of feedback that suggests they're not well thought of, or that they're lacking in authority or held in low esteem. So, no. If your only criterion is the well-being of your *boss*, then the answer might well be: *don't* say it.

Interesting isn't it, that the lens of either of those questions, smeared as it is by panic, pessimism and personal anxiety, leads you *not* to Disclose.

It's natural, of course; anything that wounds our ego can easily twist or obscure our desire for clarity. But, when we ask the slightly more objective question: "Will it help the *conversation*, if I say what I'm thinking?" the answer seems more likely to provoke the answer: "Yes. Take it on."

The less emotive, more rational side of the brain kicks in and we stay cool enough to handle the consequences.

"Come on," we're more prone to say. "Name the problem, then we can begin to deal with it." So, in the spirit of dialogue – and with the intention of getting to the bottom of things and moving them on – let's now identify two key ways to say the truth *and* make it hearable!

How to tell the truth well #1: Share your intention

When it comes to making tough things bearable to hear, this is a simple, but devastatingly effective, idea.

Essentially, sharing your intention is about saying *why* you need to say the thing *immediately* beforehand.

State clearly and carefully the *reason* for saying whatever it is first, and then (and *only* then)... say it.

Here's an example. Let's drop back into that conversation you're having with your boss, who's being talked about. (Not in a good way.)

> **"Look. I can't stand the idea of anyone overhearing negative things about themselves. It creates such a bad atmosphere and it's just a waste of everyone's time. And I think, if you can react positively to what I'm about to say, it's not too late to change how things are. So... here goes: people are talking behind your back. And they think you're a bit of a push-over."**

Now, that's still going to sting a bit – imagine hearing that as a boss – but it's not going to sting *half* as much as it would if you were to get given *only* the last two sentences:

> **"Look. People are talking behind your back. And they think you're a bit of a push-over."**

Brutal, isn't it? And, because it's so brutal, all kinds of unhelpful reactions can happen. Shock. Anger. Defensiveness. Dismissal. Denial. It's not a fun list.

"So what?" you might say. "It's out there now. Be brutal. Be direct. Let 'em have it! At least it's been said." And, yes, there's an argument for that level of directness, I suppose. But, apart from the general lack of kindness, my problem with brutal, careless honesty is that, in fact, it's *not* heard. What's heard and felt is the ferocity of attack. The impact is felt but not the substance. The dull, blunt end of a swinging hammer hits the target but the message doesn't even leave a mark. The sharper, more specific elements of criticism don't even register. And all you've done is given someone a whacking great lump on their head. This isn't feedback; it's violence.

And what about considering how to improve the Listening conditions for the boss who's on the *receiving* end of this tough feedback? How much better could they Listen, after they've been *included* in *why* certain things need to be said? It makes the truth that comes along straight afterwards much more palatable. And, because your boss understands that there's a positive intention behind it, they can allow themselves, perhaps, to hear the critique in a clearer, more purposeful way. And that's bound to result in a keener, sharper response. And, that way, someone's learning too.

So – before you deliver the news, *share your reason* for delivering it. And you'll find the truth's far easier to say.

How to tell the truth well #2: Keep it personal

So, here's the other tip on how to maximise the opportunity to give a truly honest point of view, by remembering to keep your perspective framed as just that: *your* perspective. You are only you. And that's a good thing. So highlight it. In the territory of being honest with your boss, nothing works less well than taking on the grand role of representing a world view. You walk into the world of generalisation, guesswork and hearsay, none of which tends to really cut through when it matters.

And nothing works better than explicitly giving *your* opinion. What a colleague or client will respect and Listen to is *your* take on things, especially when he or she is *told* that it's your take on things. So keep it personal.

Little phrases go a long way here. Things like:

"It seems to me as though..."

"My experience of it is that..."

"I can say only what it feels like from where I'm standing. And from where I'm standing..."

"Here's what it looks like from my point of view..."

(If you're thinking this is too simple, all I can say is that it works for me. And I honestly think it'll work for you.)

So. Represent your*self*. And no one else. Do it fully and explicitly. If you've taken enough time to come to a considered point of view, if you *know* what you think, set up your opinion purely as that. It's what *you* think, so you simply can't be wrong.

That's right. If you're sharing only *your* perspective: You. *Can't*. Be wrong.

You can be *disagreed* with. Sure. But if you're honest about what you believe, your point of view is a valid and valuable one.

Key thoughts

1. Navigate to prepare the ground for being honest. And Disclose early by putting your background into the foreground of the conversation.

2. The question to ask if you're unsure whether or not to Disclose is this: "If I say what I'm thinking, will it help the conversation?"

3. Share your intention. And keep your honesty personal. Say *why* you need to Disclose something and you'll find it easier to tell it like it is. *Own* your point of view as *your* point of view, and you can't be wrong.

A question of degree

Disclosure is often what turns a mere conversation into a true dialogue. When someone says: "Do you mind if I say what I'm really thinking?" you know things are about to go up a notch or two in interest. But honesty isn't an on or off switch. I remember recording a conversation for a podcast with the brilliant, wonderfully wild and expressive Canadian therapist, Karen Weixel-Dixon. I asked her early on in the conversation if we could have an honest conversation. "Honest?" she yelled at the top of her voice. "Honest?!" I reeled back at the ferocity of her reaction. And then she added a killer line that I often quote and will always remember, because I find it such a useful reminder of how careful to be with using absolute terms. "Honest?!" she screamed again. "How honest do you wanna *be*?!"

Chapter 10
Building

Co-creating new stuff

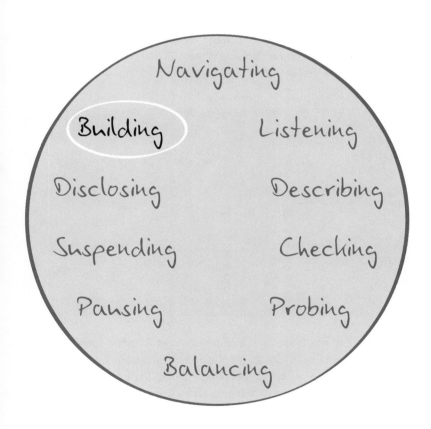

Navigating

Building

Listening

Disclosing

Describing

Suspending

Checking

Pausing

Probing

Balancing

Sometimes the reason a conversation counts more than others is that its purpose is to *create* something together. *What* you create might be any number of things:

- A new way of working.
- A solution to a problem.
- A different approach to providing a service.
- An idea that meets a set of circumstances you've not encountered before.
- A quick response to an unforeseen opportunity.

In any of these situations, and many others like them that require a collaborative conversation, Building is the skill that will unlock new ideas and possibilities that are better and richer for being the product of more minds than one.

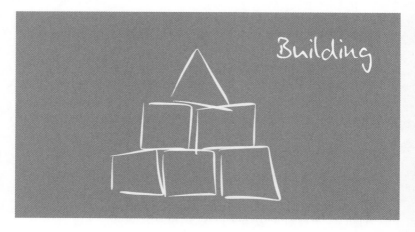

Bill Isaacs' brilliant book on dialogue, *Thinking Together*, is the best and shortest definition I know of a creative conversation. It's a rare thing, this: a conversation in which people genuinely *think* together. It's close to, but *different* from, just exchanging ideas. Because essentially it's about constructing ideas with someone else. Not just creating, *co*-creating.

The construction of ideas or solutions is such an obvious part of a creative conversation, you might wonder why it's worth considering as a skill. Why would you want to understand and put into practice something that ought to come naturally when the whole quest is to *make* something? The answer to this question is crucial and counter-intuitive, and it's this:

Building *doesn't* come naturally.

Well, not all the time, anyway.

What comes naturally is Building *your* idea. Not *the idea*, or *our* idea. We are – most of us, anyhow – inherently selfish. So we instinctively do things that get in the way of Building *with* other people. So, perhaps the best way of looking at this skill is to look at some of the very good reasons why it's tempting to do something *other* than really Build.

Ego

As I've hinted at rather heavily, I suspect that, for many of us, the biggest single thing that gets in the way of us Building in a conversation is our own ego. All of us like to think we can trump other people's ideas with our own. So, even if we're an instinctive innovator or creator – and not all of us are – it doesn't come so naturally to do it *with* other people. We perhaps like to think that we can come up with a better alternative, or a different option. But we rarely actually *say* that. Of course not. That would be rude. Instead, we revert to our old friend "code". We find the words that *allude* to or *suggest* that the previous idea was good or valuable or interesting, but actually what we *mean* is:

> **"Dismiss what he just said. Listen to me now..."**

But instead of saying it quite so bluntly, we say things like this. (Things that might *sound* like they're Building, but they're not.)

> **"That's fascinating. A really good idea in terms of how we improve performance. Let's think about that. Here's something I was wondering if we could do, though..."**

> **"I can really see how that might work... in lots of different ways. But here's an idea *I* had..."**

> **"Yes, I'm sure there are some real possibilities there... What we haven't done yet, though, is look at it *this* way..."**

These are just a few examples of something the English language is brilliant at: saying one thing but meaning another. It's not that anyone's being deliberately destructive or negative when they use these kinds of phrases. It's just that, out of politeness, we'll often make it *sound* like we're keen to further the cause of an idea that's been put on the table, but – as it happens – *we* have another one to suggest instead. *Instead*. Not as well as. Instead. And, because it's our idea, not theirs, it's important we offer it *now*. And forget the other one ever came up. It sounds a bit brutal put like this, I know. But I wouldn't mind betting you recognise what I've just Described.

New ideas: nil. Ego: one.

Mission drift

There's another reason why we don't instinctively Build with each other in conversations and why we tend to move from one idea to another too quickly. And it's about being seduced by *execution* rather than purpose. We fall in love with the potential impact something might have *way* before we really know what it *is*. Perhaps we hear something we absolutely *love* about someone's suggestion and instead of Building on it, we leap over the head of what it might actually *be* or why we might want to *do* it and land immediately into how amazing it's going to be:

"This could be incredible. I love your idea of everyone in the family owning one. I'm just seeing hundreds of people rushing to be the first in line to having one of these... It could be huge. We could generate some phenomenal PR from this. I'll call my friend Dave and get him to help with pushing it..."

This is a great example of how sometimes *positive* things like optimism, enthusiasm and energy can be just as harmful to a really important conversation as more negative traits like cynicism or pessimism. Even though the intention is good, if we get too caught up with the wrong thing, it can take us *away* from the heart of a good conversation. And, in a genuinely creative conversation, the pulse is to be found in the generation of the idea itself, not how it might be sold, cascaded or marketed.

This is a difficult pill to swallow because – let's face it – we all like positivity. It's often a desperately sought after quality in a conversation.

But it's easy to mistake generalised energy in a conversation for actual progress. Enthusiasm is a wonderful thing, but it needs to be focused in order to be useful. So hopping across the real process of Building an idea to merely applauding it creates "mission drift". You start going to places you didn't want to go to. You allow yourself to be dazzled by how things *could* be and you find the conversation loses direction and starts spinning around in a word soup of excitement. And that's not good enough. When you badly need some hard-core co-creation, you need to focus your energy where it counts most: in the *making of the idea*.

Yes, but...

And third, there's another thing that gets in the way of Building in a conversation. It's totally natural and *utterly* unhelpful. It's a counter-intuitive point this. Partly because in so many other moments in our life, it's an incredibly useful thing to do. We use it every day. It prevents us getting hurt in relationships. It stops us getting run over. And it avoids situations where we might well lose money. Sadly, however, it also stops us Building new and fabulous ideas. I'm talking here about our power to *predict*.

Prediction is part of the matrix of human intelligence. It's one of our unique strengths as a species. But weirdly, our capacity to predict can become a real problem when it comes to Building ideas or solutions. Because those two little words: "Yes, but..." are capable of such damage. And that's often where we end up with predictions. But it all happens so fast. So let's slow it down a bit. And ask what happens when we predict the outcome of an idea.

First, our mind absorbs information faster than any processor we're capable of producing in the mechanical world. So, no sooner have we heard an idea, we absorb it – or at least we *think* we do. Then, in a split second, we roll it out in a variety of imagined scenarios and assess the likely success or otherwise in a series of possible futures. As we do so, the cautious assessor in us foresees the dangers, risks and potential for failure. And no sooner do we see a problem, than we say it. So, without a thought to the impact they might have, those two little words pop out:

"Yes, but..."

And, within less than a second of an idea being forged, we're pointing out the things that could go wrong with it. Very few ideas are perfect when first expressed. And you can find fault with almost anything when it's at the hatching stage. So, no matter how good an idea is, pretty much *any* possibility is likely to come with a few reasons for it *not* to work. The question is, do we choose to allow such intense scrutiny so early on? And if not... what do we do instead?

Remedies

So, what are the easy shifts we can make to Build more successfully?

First, to address the ego question: the most significant shift you can make is to move from *my* idea to *our* idea. After all, if you're co-creating, it doesn't matter who initiates the idea. The point is how good can we *make* it. So, experiment with taking credit out of the equation. Serve the cause. Even if you think an idea isn't that good, park your alternative for a few minutes and go with what's on the table. (If the idea isn't a good one, that'll soon become apparent.)

If you have another idea... Great! Just acknowledge it openly:

> **"You've just prompted an idea in my head. Wait! Let me scribble it down. And then let's get back to yours so we can look at how it might work in practice. We can look at my idea later."**

(It sounds so obvious put in black and white, but it's rare to hear anything like this happen.)

Second, there's the tendency we have to drift off course and stop actually creating the idea. This is partly about the other skill of Navigating that will help you stay in the right place to Build. Just a quick reminder that the *purpose* of the conversation goes a long way:

> **"Hang on, let's remember we're here to create a new structure. Let's stick with that. As tempting as it is to imagine now what the implications might be when it's done, let's take a step back and work on how we can make this a practical plan..."**

And third, how do we counter the "Yes, but..." mentality?

There's a very simple answer to that.

"Yes, and..."

Be rigorous. Every time you feel your instinct to be cautious, rise up and predict problems come to the fore, bite your tongue and say "Yes, and..." You'll be amazed what comes out of your mouth next. Of course I'm not suggesting you do this indiscriminately, but try accepting whatever comes your way. It'll feel strange, thrilling and, most importantly, you'll experience for yourself what Building really means: taking a risk.

Key thoughts

1. Put your ego to one side. You're not as important as the best idea is.

2. Don't be seduced by how big the impact might be in the future. *Make it good. Now. And here.*

3. Say "Yes, and..."

Saplings

Jonny Ives, the co-inventor of the iPod, talks brilliantly about Building. He says that when ideas are new, they're like seedlings: fragile, fresh and easily destroyed. So we should be careful about where and how we tread. Let's briefly revisit that moment I mentioned in the chapter on Suspending, when Ives first suggested the concept of the iPod. Someone at some point must have said something like: "Okay. Let's say we can invent something that can hold a gazillion songs. What if it had a screen? So we could watch videos on it? And play games? In fact, what if we could build all of these things... into a phone?"

Part 2
The Situations

Navigating

Building

Listening

Disclosing

Describing

Suspending

Checking

Pausing

Probing

Balancing

How, when and where to apply the skills

Having introduced you to the 10 core skills of conversation, it's time now to move into the second part of this book. The section where we put these skills to work in a variety of situations.

In each of the chapters that follow, I've sketched out some relatively common situations and suggested which skills might help most, when and where.

There is no order. No sequence of complexity. You can read these chapters one by one in sequence, or dip into them however you like. Perhaps there's a situation that's especially relevant to you. If so – go to it first; my hope is that a particular chapter will help you immediately.

But I hope, too, that you'll be sufficiently curious to read beyond whatever your urgent need might be, if only for this reason: sometimes, we have an instinctively negative *reaction* to a certain type of work situation. Maybe it feels difficult. Awkward. Uncomfortable. Or we just don't *like* it. We certainly don't look forward to it. But, rather than explore *why* we feel the way we do about it, we put our head down, avoid it for as long as possible and, only when it becomes totally unavoidable, we reluctantly shuffle into it, hoping it won't last long. We hold low hopes for it being anything other than grim. We may even get a bit tense and snappy before it. And, by the time we actually get to have it, we've stored up a whole load of reasons why it's not going to go well or even be worth having.

The conversation's not even happened yet and we already resent it. But the odd thing is, we're not really sure *why*. So, we reach out for a reason. And more often than not, that search becomes a quest for something (or someone) to *blame*. We pin the nature of the problem onto something unchangeable. A person, perhaps. Or a set of circumstances. Because, if we can pin the blame elsewhere, then at least we can avoid any hope of changing it:

> "I find those formal feedback sessions so clunky and false. All that sitting in a chair close to each other..."

We might even give one of these situations – or ourselves – a label, which makes us think of it as even more of a fixed point; an unchangeable state of affairs:

"I'm just not good in those situations."

"It's a sales pitch. I'm no good at sales."

"I'm a coward when it comes to big group sessions."

If you have thoughts like this in your head, I'd like to suggest two things to you. First, the situation you're dreading *isn't* as dreadful as you think. It's *just* a conversation. It's not a war. It's not a court case. And it's certainly not a nightmare. It's a conversation. A conversation that you can handle.

The second thing to say is that you *can* affect the outcome of that conversation. You can influence it. You can change it. All you need to do is apply yourself.

If you like a mantra, try this one for size:

There's no such thing as an unhave-able conversation. And there's no such thing as an impossible situation.

(Don't get me wrong. Some situations are incredibly tough. But nothing's too tough to talk about.)

So, with that in mind, let me introduce you to Part 2, The Situations. In preparing this list of skills and situations, I confess to being a little selective. In most situations, *all* of the skills are important, or at least they could be. But I do want to keep each chapter to a digestible size. So, in each case I've chosen mostly to focus on bringing to bear the most relevant three or four skills in particular.

So – use this next part of the book as you will. Search for the situation that's staring you in the face right now. And consider how, by saying what you need to about it, you're taking the first vital steps towards solving it. Whatever it is, you're more than capable of sorting it out.

Chapter 11
I'd be perfect
for you

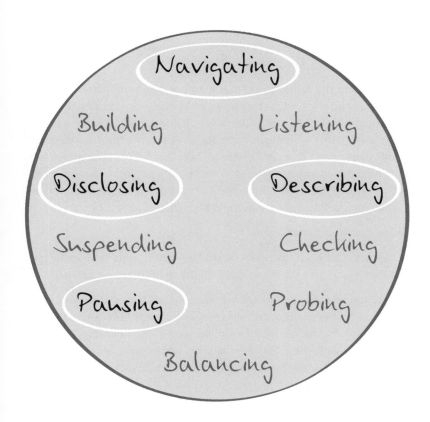

Getting the job

A job interview can often bring out the worst in us. Just when we need to show the best of us.

The build up can be fairly horrendous. We get anxious. We decide in advance that it won't go well. Friends try to help by telling us it'll be fine. Or, even worse, they say with utter certainty: "You'll be brilliant!" (How do they know?) And, of course, their encouragement and advice comes from a good place, but it's often the last thing we need. It's hopelessly general and as likely to be wrong as right. So we ask around for advice. And it pours in, usually based on other people's experiences – not ours. So, by the time we get to the actual interview, we have so many voices in our head, the only feelings we can genuinely call our own are confusion and a fear of being tongue-tied.

We walk into the room, trying to remember a hundred different things but, of course, any kind of strategy we've carefully devised deserts us and any hopes we had of showing ourselves off in a good light seem a million miles away. Now all we can hope for is to survive the trauma of the whole experience. Our confidence is shot. Our nerves take over. We've long abandoned any aspirations to be at our best. Just getting out alive seems like a good option. So, as our name is called, we cross our fingers behind our back and put ourselves in the hands of fate.

Tell you what. Let's start again.

In fact, let's tear down the whole fearful construction that's so easily built around the idea of a job interview and look again at what it actually *is*.

Behind the anxieties and imagined scenarios of how an interview might go lies... a conversation. A conversation with a clear purpose: to find the right person for the job in question. Someone who's capable. Someone who'll fit in with the other people who work there. Someone who'll perhaps bring in some fresh ideas. Someone who'll work hard. Someone who won't leave after a few weeks. Someone who, in some way, will inject something new and valuable to the place of work.

That's all it is. A conversation with a purpose.

Now, it's a conversation where the stakes are high, of course, because there's a very specific and important outcome: a job. But it's still a conversation. And, while naturally a good deal of whether you get the job will be down to whether you've got the right skills for it, if you're far enough through the process to get an interview, the chances are that how you *perform* in that conversation about the job will have a significant influence on whether you get it or not.

And given that (as tends to be the case) there are more people than just you with the capabilities to do the job, then, if the people who are interviewing you get a strong sense in a short time that you're someone they can engage with, who Listens, who responds well to a challenge, they're bound to look more favourably on you as a candidate. Put another way, if you can capture their interest, if you can make them think, if you can give them an experience that's distinctive and unique, you'll start to shift their perceptions of you from "the next interviewee" towards "someone we want to work with".

And the fundamental thing you can change to make this possible is to change the conversation from the usual repetitive tennis match that forms the basis of many job interviews:

1. Take a seat.

2. Question asked.

3. Question answered.

4. Question asked.

5. Question answered.

6. Question asked.

7. Question answered.

8. Thank you. We'll let you know.

I'm not disputing for a moment that questions will be part of the interview. Of course they'll ask questions. And of course you'll give answers. But, rather than totally submitting to a Them versus Me format that can make it feel like an interrogation, it's within your gift to influence the type of conversation it is. Instead of playing into the space of conversational ping-pong by giving a standard reply and then waiting for the next question, you can make the 30 minutes or so of the conversation *far* more interesting. And all you need to do is apply a few of the basic principles and skills of having a good conversation.

How? Let's focus on a few simple things.

Take responsibility for making the *Time and Space* for your interview feel more like a joint effort, a collaborative conversation, by *Navigating*. Remember, Navigating is about how you manage the *journey* of a conversation. Keep it on course and collective. Make it an us thing, not a you and me thing. And make sure you don't wander off in one direction whilst your fellow travellers go off in another. Navigating promotes a useful kind of equality in the conversation, where it feels like you're both there for the same reason.

(Which of course you are — you're both there to find the best person for the job.)

Let's look at a specific example of how Navigating can help you in an interview situation:

Say you get asked a question, which as we know tends to be what happens in an interview! Don't just blurt out a reply until you run out of steam. Share with them, simply, how you want to respond to the question and keep them *with* you on the map of your answer:

> **"Okay. How about I give you an overview first of what my old company was really focused on and then get into a couple of examples to illustrate what I did most of in my old job?"**

They know what to expect now. You're literally keeping them on the journey with you. And because they know where you're going, they're much less likely to interrupt you, just when you don't want them to.

Or, of course... by suggesting a route for your answer, you might have helped them to steer *with* you a little bit. They might, for example, come back and say something like:

"Actually, we know plenty about your old company. We have some pretty strong links with them. Let's get straight into the examples. That'd be really helpful for us..."

Even better. The language of Navigating is usefully infectious. Once *they're* using phrases like "Why don't we..." or even just the word "Let's..." you know you're on the journey of the conversation together.

The next really useful skill in this context is *Disclosing*. Sharing what you're really thinking. This is a great enabler in an interview because it makes you less of a stranger in the midst. You Disclose with people you trust. And it shows in you a quality that's surely a fundamental requirement of any job: your comfort with honesty. So, here's an apparent contradiction: be confident enough to be vulnerable. Honesty is an attractive quality. So get it out there. And remember, what helps you to say the honest thing, is first to say *why* you want to say it. So let's imagine that to give a really good Description of an experience you've had, you need to reveal a few little-known facts. Facts that might be sensitive...

"I'm happy to tell you exactly how it was for me. If you can treat this confidentially. But there are a few reasons why it might sound a bit clumsy. First of all, I've not talked about it much openly. And second, it's a subject that's close to my heart so I want to make sure you get a full appreciation of what really happened. Here goes: It was the toughest time of anyone's professional life, I think..."

Honesty makes for compelling story telling. So Disclosing is nearly always a powerful thing to do. And a sense that you're being really honest will change the temperature of a conversation. It makes it real. Authentic. It's a way to show that you're a genuine person with genuine points of view, views that you give a damn about. So go for it. But help the interviewer to hear what you're Disclosing in the right frame. A bit of Navigating will help you here, too...

"Well, it's not a rosy picture. Can I be frank with you about why?"

So now they have a choice. They can Navigate with you and say yes, go ahead, Disclose away:

"Yes, please do. We'll treat anything you say here with the utmost respect and it won't go any further."

Or they can Navigate with you and effectively say: "Sure, Disclose. But no more than you need to."

"We don't need to know names or numbers. Just help us understand what it was really like for you to deal with the challenges you faced. That's what we're really interested in."

Again, that last phrase is interesting. They're telling you what they really need to know. (Disclosing is infectious, too!)

There's a final tip on making an interview into a conversation and it's about how you use the skills of *Describing* and *Pausing*.

Time to think

In a finite amount of time, it pays to take *care* with your words. Choose them carefully. Take your time. Invest energy in finding the right set of words:

"What would I say were my strengths as a leader?"

Take time to Pause. (But let them know that's what you're doing. Then it won't feel like a tense Pause.)

"Interesting question. Can I take just a second or two? I want to give you a helpful answer."

You've bought time to think. And you've Disclosed nicely, too. Well done. A better answer will come as a result:

"I think... I think I Listen well. And then, once I've Listened, I'll make a clear decision. And take responsibility for it."

Key thoughts

1. Create a positive sense of *Time and Space*. And *Navigate* with your interviewer to make it a conversation. Make it a shared journey.

2. Be honest by *Disclosing*. And help yourself and them by giving the background as to why you *want* to be honest.

3. Take time and *Pause* if you need to in order to *Describe* things really well.

Chapter 12
You'd be perfect for us

Navigating

Building

Listening

Disclosing

Describing

Suspending

Checking

Pausing

Probing

Balancing

Giving the job

It won't be news to you if I say that finding the right person for a job is a crucial part of running a strong, growing business.

But it might be a new idea that having a better conversation when you're interviewing, could save your business a fortune.

Get the right man or woman at the right time, and your business, large or small, can get a significant boost. But employ someone who's not right, someone who, in spite of all kinds of healthy and constructive feedback conversations, just doesn't turn out to do the job well, or is in some way wrong for where you work, well that's a different story. You'll get a poor return on your investment. You'll agitate and irritate the people who've worked for you for a long time. You'll have to go through the discomfort and pain of letting someone go – a horrible thing to go through, on all sides. And then you'll have to enter back into the costly and time-hungry process of finding someone else!

So a *lot* of cost in terms of money, energy, time and pain is created easily by the consequences of a choice made after just one or maybe two conversations. Interviews are conversations that can count for a great deal.

It's not a hard job then, I hope, to convince you that it's worth thinking a little harder about how well that particular kind of conversation might go, from the potential employer's side. Because how *you* are in this conversation is hugely influential on how your candidate is.

Do it right, and you can enable and encourage them to be articulate, honest and (frankly) just really helpful. Do it wrong and you could easily assist in helping someone to get a job who really ought not to. And, in turn of course, you might overlook someone who'd be much better at the job than you could imagine.

So, how can you best discover if they are or *aren't* the right person for the job by influencing the conversation you have with them? And what can you do to *help* interviewees represent themselves well?

Why does it go wrong?

Let's look first at the two main reasons for the wrong candidate getting a job.

1. The candidate wants the job, regardless of whether they are right for it.

2. You want someone to succeed or fail. Before you've even interviewed them.

In both instances, the conversation that sits at the heart of the decision gets distorted. The desperate candidate glides over, or avoids, talking about his or her weaknesses. The hopeful interviewer warps his or her perception to fit their deepest wish that this candidate has what it takes. At least one hidden agenda creeps into the process and the conversation falls victim to its own keenly desired (but undisclosed) outcomes...

Not a very healthy state of affairs. And one that's unlikely to produce the best person for the job in hand.

So what do you need to do more of?

At its simplest, a better conversation leads to a better interview. And in this context, a better conversation means one that creates real insight, that gets behind the obvious, that stimulates some in-the-moment thinking and encourages plenty of straight talking. And, if you just look after and pay attention to the right components of that conversation, you'll find it much harder to get it wrong. And much easier to get it right.

Time and Space

First, it's your job as the interviewer to create the right sense of *Time and Space* to help the conversation be as good as it can be. If you want to come to a point of judgement about the individual who's going to walk into the room, then it's only fair to judge a good version of them. So, enable them to be as relaxed and as confident as they can realistically be. Prepare them to be in a good place for a great conversation. Position their chair somewhere they're not going to be distracted by the outside world or movement. Book a room that's quiet. Maybe sit in their seat to look at the lighting before they come in and make sure that lamp isn't shining in their eye. If you show consideration for the person you're interviewing, they'll sense that you're dedicating some real attention to them as an individual. And they'll become a better candidate.

Navigate and Disclose

Now – when it comes to the actual conversation, let's look first at how *Navigating* and *Disclosing* can help you.

And let's think about helping the candidate to help you. You want honest answers and real insight. What you don't want is the candidate worrying about the wrong things or guessing what you might be digging around for. So, treat them as your partner in conversation. Let them know roughly what the scope of the conversation's going to be. Keep them with you on the journey – not as a wary passenger on an unpredictable road of twists and turns but as a participant. Someone who's going to help you steer a good course and serve the same purpose as you. Tell them why you want to ask what you want to ask. Help them understand what kind of answers you want. What does this sound and look like?

Well, it's the difference between a question like this:

> **"If you could change one thing about your career so far, what would it be?"**

Nothing wrong with that as a question. Except that the poor candidate has no idea why you're asking it. So they'll expend a whole lot of energy trying to work it out. Whereas, if you Navigate and Disclose a bit first...

> **"Let's start with a nice big open question and then we'll get more specific about the role in a while. We're big on being a learning culture here. Mistakes happen. They're forgivable. But the worst kind of mistake is not to learn when you mess up. So... I know it's a big question to open up with but, if you could change one thing about your career so far, what would it be?"**

It's a big difference. You can see and hear, I hope, that now the interviewee is being *included* in the thinking. They're on the journey. They're informed. And they have a notion both of the purpose *and* the position of the question. Which means they're more likely to give an answer that will be honest, useful and interesting.

A few gentler Navigating and Disclosing nudges along the way can help, too. Things that invite a shared responsibility for the direction of the conversation. Things like:

> **"We'll make sure there's time for you to ask about the business at the end. So, for now, let's just give you a chance to tell us about you. How's that for a starter?"**

> **"I'd like to ask some quick questions that dart around a bit. Just so I can build up a picture of how you are in different situations. Short answers will help us get through as much territory as possible. Sound okay?"**

Or:

> **"Right. I'd like to understand more about the kind of person you are outside of work. We have time for three more questions if we're both fairly concise, or we could dive into one big one. Which shall we go for?"**

(Remember: better questions get better answers.)

Listen and Probe

Next, comes the quality of *Listening* as an interviewer. If you can Listen really well in an interview, you'll learn so much more than just what's being said. It's the business of Listening for small things. Those tiny indicators that something is worth pursuing and *Probing*, because it's significant to the person you're in conversation with.

It might be that they repeat or *lean* on a particular word...

> **"There was once a small problem we had. Where no one really knew what to do. Because it was unfamiliar. It was unique. Yes. *Unique*. That was a really testing time."**

A good Probe here simply would be to repeat the word again...

"Unique?"

This is often enough to bring out a richer explanation like this...

"Utterly unique. We discovered that it wasn't enough to trust the methodologies we all knew. We had to take a risk. And we weren't used to doing that."

Or perhaps they Pause before a certain phrase:

"Only three of us had been in the business for longer than six months and we... (PAUSE) That was when we really found out who we were."

All you have to do to bring out more here and Probe is notice that it happened to bring out more. And soften your enquiry with that golden word:

"That was an interesting little Pause..."

And let them do the rest:

"Well – it was an interesting time. I've never known people work so hard. But, at the same time, have so much energy..."

Or maybe there's an obvious word that seems ready to come... and they choose to say something else.

"The budget had been spent. The ideas had dried up. We had one more chance. You know. A last... Yes, tough times."

There's a word that seems missing. So, if you're Listening carefully enough, you can Probe lightly by drawing attention to it. There's more than likely something there.

"It felt like you were going to say 'last stand' then..."

You'll soon know if you've hit the mark...

"I was! But... well, we weren't exactly standing. We were down and out already. We'd been sold. But no one knew."

So, Listen and Probe for richer, more meaningful content.

Suspend and Describe

If you want to look beyond the obvious, if you want to be potentially surprised by someone, you need to get used to Suspending your judgement when you're interviewing. Obviously at some point *after* the conversation you'll need to make a judgement on whether they're the person you want. But don't confuse the decision with the process. It may well be that we're put off by small signals early on in a conversation that aren't as significant as we think.

Often we're not even looking for the person we need. And we don't even realise that someone is the right person until we've looked at things from a different angle. So, if you can Listen with an open mind, you'll be doing your interviewee a huge favour and quite possibly, uncovering a new way of thinking for you about the role in question.

And finally a quick word here about the skill of Describing.

In an interview, the words you choose will be heard and magnified. Your language and the way you use it will have a big impact on this new, fresh and hungry Listener. So, think carefully and consider the words you use. Be simple. Be clear. Be concise. Be compelling.

And in the spirit of great conversation, allow yourself to explore *new* ways of saying things. Bring a fresh feel for yourself to the familiar territory you're Describing. Challenge yourself to make what you and your business do sound genuinely interesting. Use real-life examples, stories, and anecdotes. The more compelling your vision and your way of talking and Listening, the more likely you are to attract the best people to work with you.

Key thoughts

1. Give to your interviewee a sense of *Time and Space*. Don't rush them. Make them feel *comfortable*.

2. *Navigate* to keep them with you. *Disclose* to keep them honest.

3. *Listen* to hear the small things. *Probe* to find out more. And *Describe* in order to compel.

Chapter 13
Good call

Time to make some decisions

In a fantasy world, all of our work conversations would be rich, thorough and constructive. Each seam of the subject in question would be carefully and comprehensively mined from top to bottom; every ounce of valuable insight and opinion extracted as we comprehensively explore whatever territory it is we've agreed to dig around in.

And most importantly of all, we'd always make the right decisions as a result. We'd constantly *say it and solve it* brilliantly. Every time.

But it doesn't quite work like that, does it?

It might be our *wish* to look in every nook and cranny, to make sure we've genuinely considered every single possibility before making the choices we need to make, but the reality is that mostly we don't.

Or can't.

Why?

Well, there are two main hurdles to making good choices: time and information. And there are ways of making sure that, by having a good conversation and making the most of what you have, you make better decisions.

Timely choices

Let's look at time first. It's usually cited as the biggest obstacle to making a good choice. No one has enough of it. And we could all do with more of it.

I've witnessed a lot of decisions in a lot of workplaces. And I've been part of making them happen sometimes. Some have been good. Others not. But nearly all of them been made under time pressure. And, when the decisions have been shown to be poor, people have often blamed the need to make a choice without sufficient thinking time.

But here's something I've noticed. In just about *every* situation I can recall, it's not that there has *never* been the time to make a thorough decision. It's because the time available was poorly used. An event with a six-month lead-time is cobbled together in the last six weeks. A carefully constructed preparation timeline of six days gets ignored. Or a perfectly decent timeframe of three weeks to set up a project has been slowly eroded. So the days or weeks pass. The deadline looms. The stress builds. Things get rushed. Money gets wasted. And choices get made in a hurry.

So it's more about tim*ing* than time. If you've had enough time but you've run *out* of it, somewhere, at some point, a good conversation's been missing. And, if we know time is always short, whether it's 12 weeks or 2 days, we can make much better use of the hours we *have* by consciously having better, more thorough conversations.

Let's debunk a myth here. Some people think that having a thorough conversation takes up too much time; that it's an unaffordable activity. And that, when push comes to shove, you just need to cut to the chase and make somewhat less careful, more aggressive decisions. Maybe they're right, maybe they're wrong. But at least they're decisions. And no more time is wasted.

Wrong. Wrong. And wrong.

Great conversations *save* time. You'll make much better decisions and choices if you have a good conversation about them. If you're putting on a conference, for instance, *say it and solve it* early on and you'll waste less time pursuing the wrong venues, guest speakers you'd like but don't have the budget for and making film clips that will never get shown. Or, if you're reorganising your shop, your surgery or studio, have the crucial conversations *earlier* than you might first think and you'll find yourself creating ideas that you wouldn't if you were already up against a deadline. Like, for example, making a miniature model of the space you're about to adapt, so you can try things out physically and at a small scale without going to the cost of trying out a real sofa, chairs or table. Put a conversation like that off until nearer the move, and you'll find yourself buying expensive furniture that doesn't fit or you don't like and wasting time reordering, waiting or trying to make round pegs (or chairs) fit into a square hole (or hall).

(Up the ante on the quality of the conversation and you'll save bags of time.)

But you can save time, too, when you're *having* the conversation. A really good conversation is one where you get further, faster *and* deeper more quickly. Where the choices you make are more thorough. And where you spend less time tentatively dipping your toes into the water and instead plunging deep into where it matters most.

Informed choices

But, if a conversation is about making choices, you need to know those choices are being made based on solid, reliable information. You can talk for a long time about options a, b and c but, if you've not tested and understood what those options really mean, you might as well draw straws. No amount of time spent can replace good *information*. Information comes in all shapes and sizes. Let's look at just a few bits of what I'd call the grittier examples of information:

- **Market conditions.** How much are people spending on what, that kind of thing.

- **Accurate sales figures.** How much are you selling, to whom, when and why.

- **Rich research on your customers.** What kind of people use your service or products.

- **Up-to-date statistics on consumer trends.** What else are people doing with themselves.

- **Meaningful website data.** More than hitting on you, who's actually engaging with you online.

- **Well-sourced staff surveys.** What are your people saying about you and anything else.

- **Transparent safety records.** What goes wrong, who gets hurt and why.

All of these things will tell you a lot of what you need to know. Hardcore information. Numbers and statistics. Numbers and statistics that should be informing your decisions.

Then, there are the other, less tangible forms of information that can be equally important, if a little less directly correlated:

- **Changes in the law.** Adapting to shifts in legal working practice.

- **The "feel" of the workplace.** How good or bad people feel about working for you.

- **Special events.** Royal ones, sporting ones, national ones, local ones.

- **Weather forecast.** See below.

- **Fashion.** What colours, shapes and kinds of design are current and attractive to people *this* Spring?

Again, there's a wide range in just a few examples, this time of the "softer" variety that might well affect the choices you make for your business. (Try being an ice-cream seller in Blackpool on a cold, wet and windy day in July.) So, almost without looking, we *know* there's a lot of information out there.

But in a *poor* conversation, it's *only* this kind of information that's referred to – the sort that's immediately available. It's overly trusted in terms of reliability. It's over-weighted in terms of its relevance. And it's used to back up previously held points of view rather than provoke new ones. In a conversation that *counts*, information is well-sourced, intelligently challenged and interrogated for substance, relevance and new possibilities.

So, what I'm suggesting is simply this: when choices need to be made, when there's a lot riding on the outcomes of a conversation, there are some key questions we ought to be asking and some powerful conversational muscles to flex in order to answer those questions.

The question is: which muscles do we flex? Or which buttons do we press to make the better choices and decisions, to get the richer information and use the time we have most effectively?

Here are the skills that will do the business in this context.

Navigate

At the beginning of a conversation, be explicit about what you're here to do. Not just about the time you have to do it in. If you know what kind of a conversation you need, it's essential to say so:

> **"We need to go one way or the other today. So let's keep that in mind. This is not about wishful thinking. It's about making our minds up. Let's not allow each other to get away with saying anything we can't really follow through on. Agreed?"**

And, if you sharply define the territory and purpose of the conversation at the outset, you'll make it much harder for any slippage to creep in. And, even when it *does*, if you've agreed how you want to go about things clearly at the beginning, it's so much easier to remind people and adjust the tiller as you go along:

> **"It feels to me like in the last few minutes we've started to drift into wishing budgets were different. They're not. Let's stay hard and fast on where we can cut expenditure. We'll find time afterwards to think a bit more creatively about how to address any holes we think are exposed. For now, let's focus on where we can save money. Yes?"**

Disclose

Simply telling it like it is will save you a lot of time. And there's nothing better than a good dose of obscurity if you want to *waste* it. So if you think that code and half-told truths are a legitimate part of moving on a conversation towards making a choice, please think again. Or at least consider the *quality* of choice you're making more likely by being partial with the truth.

I've Listened to, and heard, many people try to fashion an agreement that will bring about a final decision. The phrases that crop up in situations like these are as transparent as they are dangerous. If someone admits to being careful with what they say, if they talk about the importance of *keeping people on board* or saying that, while there may be differences they think *broadly* we're in agreement... pay special attention to the need for honesty. And ask for them to say what they're *really* thinking, respectfully. Start by walking your talk:

"Let me be frank with you..."

Many people dislike this kind of phrase. They say things like: "Just say it!" "Spit it out." Or "Don't ask for permission, just speak up!" My take is that there's often value in giving a little warning that you're about to Disclose more than you might have done. It gives people a chance to prepare themselves to Listen to a calm, measured call for candour:

"This is a serious decision we're making. So let's be clear and explicit. Say what you're thinking. If we disagree, we disagree! We'll work it out. But let's not slip into subtly covering up what we believe and trying to disguise a genuine disagreement as some kind of false accord..."

These kinds of requests for honesty require courage, but they're the kind of sharp incisions that cut to the quick of a conversation that counts; they make them real, genuine and authentic. And thereby far more likely to create solid, dependable decisions.

Check

When you're making decisions, it's crucial to be thorough about what's being said and not said. So Check what someone means before you decide if you're for it or against it. If it's make-your-mind-up time, it's important that everyone understands exactly what's being proposed:

"So, let me be clear. You're saying, reduce the staff count by 10 per cent. That's less than we said a few minutes ago. But offer a pay rise to the people we keep?"

The response will do one of two things, both of which are good. You'll either get confirmation that you heard it right, or you'll create an opportunity for a correction. Both of which increase the quality of the conversation; the second of which guarantees that, even if you heard it wrong initially, you're going to hear it right now.

Probe

So here's the skill that's made to test the quality of the information you have, so you can make the best possible choices. You need the *good* stuff. And great questions are the way to get it.

Short, sharp questions will help you here:

- Are we sure those facts are right?

- Where did we get those numbers from?

- Does everyone understand these figures?

- Is the source reliable?

- What does this tell us?

- What's the important part of this data?

- Where should we be looking here?

- Which numbers are going to tell us most?

When it's time to go one way or the other, ambiguity is not good company. An awareness of how to really Probe in a conversation will avoid a situation where important choices are being made based on only *some* of the information. Be exhaustive. Be thorough. Be accurate.

Key thoughts

1. Interrogate your information with great questions. *Check* often and *Probe* sharply.

2. You know time is short, so be rigorous with how you use it. *Navigate* to avoid drifting off topic.

3. Remember that a great conversation *saves* time, so invest in it by *Disclosing* what you *really* think.

Chapter 14
Just a couple
of thoughts
for you

Giving good feedback

Luckily, none of us is perfect. At work or anywhere else. We're all capable of more, of improving and refining the way we perform at work. And, as a dear friend said to me once: the day we stop learning is the day we stop living.

So, giving feedback at work, talking *now* because it'll help us to do better next time, should be a healthy part of our everyday experience. Reflecting on how we've done something, looking at how we can do it better, and moving on to the next thing... this should be the bread and butter of our working practice. But often, sadly, it's not. And from what I've noticed, there are three main reasons why:

1. We're too busy getting on with the next thing to look back at what we just did.

2. We think of feedback as something someone *else* does to *us*; it's not something we need to initiate.

3. We don't actually want it. Or think we need it. And anyway: "I'm doing fine."

And, if you're the person who could be *giving* the feedback, there are good reasons to avoid it from that angle as well:

1. You're too busy to give feedback in a regular way. Anyway, that's what six-monthly reviews are for.

2. The only feedback you have is difficult. Either it's too personal or too negative. It's too awkward.

3. There's no particular need to give feedback. They don't want it. And anyway: "They're doing fine."

So, the enemies of feedback conversations are many and various. Bigger companies have now institutionalised it into formal annual reviews, which can mean we don't feel it's our own duty to take on other people's feedback in between times. At a personal level, we're busy. Too busy to take time to reflect and find out how well or not we're doing. And then there's the old "If it ain't broke, why fix it?" mentality. Which means you get to hear feedback only when things go wrong. (And you miss out on chances to consider *why* what you're doing is working!)

I won't stack up a huge wall of arguments for more frequent, day-to-day feedback conversations. All I'll say is that teams and organisations I've worked with that get close to fulfilling their potential, the workplaces that thrive and grow, the businesses that hold onto and develop their best people *all* value good-quality feedback. And the feedback conversation doesn't wait six months for a review date – it happens when it needs to happen. It doesn't get delayed because things are busy – it's habitual, sensitive, quick and lightly done. And, finally – and here's what gets me excited – *all* it is, is a conversation. A healthy, productive, powerful cocreating conversation.

So. Case made. (I hope.)

Let's get on and look at which skills can *help* you have this particular breed of conversation. Because *how* you give feedback has a dramatic impact on whether you have it or not. If your experience of it – on either side – is a positive one, then of course you're likely to do it again. If a feedback conversation goes badly, it can hurt enough to avoid it at all costs.

(For what it's worth, I've seen badly handled feedback cause more upset in the workplace than anything else.)

Navigate

Remember that one of the key benefits of Navigating is that it keeps a conversation safe. And a feedback conversation *needs* to feel safe *because* it might be a little personal; there'll probably be an element of criticism present and, as human beings, often we react to being told we're not as good as we could have been. So an awareness of the type of conversation you both want to have is crucial.

It's about Describing the journey before you set off.

So, if you're *giving* feedback, start with something like:

> **"Okay – so you asked me to be honest and I have two main things I think I can be usefully tough with you about. But I have some really positive stuff for you to hear. And I want to give that to you now. Before. So long as you Listen. Because the positive stuff is**

as important as the criticism you'll get in a minute or two. You've made progress and I want you to hear it. Okay?"

Forewarned is forearmed. Your colleague can prepare to take on the difficult things but also, hopefully, still will hear what else you have to say to them.

Disclose

Honesty in a feedback conversation is totally essential. It's a hard enough conversation to have anyway, because it's got a ring of "a more honest conversation" about it, even before it's happened. (Perhaps that's another reason why some people dread them!) So *be* honest. Be sensitive, but be honest. Not just about what's wrong. But about what's right, too. Make it personal – and you'll make it meaningful.

Compare this accurate, but impersonal, way of feeding back:

"You're hitting the scores we want you to. So that's good. And you seem to have a low sick day rate. And you're well thought of in the team. You need to improve on your timeliness, though. You've been late 6 days out of the last 30. What's going on there?"

And then *this* way:

"So, your numbers are just about where I'd like them to be – I'm not surprised about that. But I'm glad you've not had an early drop off, that means to me you're motivated by the targets. I'm worried, though, about the lateness. It feels odd to me. You're never sick but you're often late. I wonder what's going on?"

Just a few small Disclosing elements make a difference. Using the I word more. Saying how things make you *feel* and *think* (not surprised, glad, worried, feeling odd, wondering...) These are potent, small but significant acts of Disclosure. And they'll encourage the same thing in response.

Describe

The words you choose to use are really important in a feedback conversation. Take your time to find the right ones. In a conversation like this, where it's important to locate exactly where someone *is* (what they're thinking and feeling), you should encourage and practise being specific and accurate, not general and imprecise.

Again, compare these two ways of talking about why something's been difficult:

> **"Yes, the lateness thing. Life's been busy, you know, outside work. There's a fair bit of pressure. Just family stuff, you know. And so, sometimes, I... just end up being late. I'm sorry. I'm really sorry. It'll get better soon, I promise."**

All this might be true. But you're not really sharing anything in a way that's going to penetrate with someone Listening. Someone who may well *want* to understand what's going on.

If you Describe things more specifically, more completely and clearly, you'll be able to share what things are like for you:

> **"I'm sorry. Let me tell you what's happening. My partner isn't sleeping well. And we don't know why. So I'm helping out with the childcare as much as I can in the mornings so she gets at least a few hours. I've made arrangements to get help. But it won't change until next week."**

Being *specific*. That's what Describing is about:

> **"I think I need support on-the-job with the technical side of things. I tend to learn much more quickly when I'm in a live process."**

And if you're giving feedback, point to real *examples*:

> **"You were so sharp in the August meeting. Quick to respond. Really well prepared. And you asked great questions."**

Listen, Suspend and Check

And, finally, these three skills are enormously useful used together in a feedback conversation. Try Listening without prejudice. Listen for the underlying message. Have an open mind. Suspend your knowledge of what you think is true, the historical bit of your brain that will rule out things you've not heard before. And then Check to make sure what you've heard is what was meant.

> "So – this is unusual for me to be picked up on planning. I'm normally pretty good in this area. But I want to take this on, so... Let me make sure I understand. It's more about how I relate to *customers*, how I talk to *them* about our range of services, than how thorough I am giving reports to the staff here each month? You're saying I'm not as clear with customers as I am with the team?"

This is a great way to absorb feedback: play it back. In different words. And you'll begin to hear new things, new ways in which you can improve.

How was it for you?

And here's the final tip on feedback conversations. Make a habit of Checking in with your colleagues or coworkers at the end of a feedback conversation. Treat it like a health check. Before you leave each other's company, just step out of the content for a minute and take it in turns to give the conversation a mini review. Good bits. Bad bits. Interesting bits and boring bits. Acknowledge that things were tricky back there. Ask how it was for them. Have a look *together* at what's been achieved. Find your own words, but the kind of thing I mean is something like this:

> "Thanks for that. It felt to me like we were getting pretty close to the bone a couple of times there. But we stuck to our guns, even when it came to dealing with those uncomfortable truths. And, as far as I'm concerned, that edginess was worth it. We've made two decisions about things I can change immediately and we've opened up a whole new area for me to look at. I sense there's a way to go yet. But I'm really clear now on what my priorities should be.

What do you think? How was it for you? Are you comfortable with how that went and where we are now?"

By the way, with questions like these at the end, make sure you give your partner in conversation *time* to answer them. This isn't politeness; it's hard-core performance management and relationship building.

Sooner or later, if you're rigorous, it'll become a habit. Until it does, be disciplined and deliberate in making it happen.

If you can confidently not just have, but review, your feedback conversations, if you can make a habit of *making time* for them, you'll enjoy three invaluable things with whoever it is you work with:

1. Mutual clarity on where you both are now, on what the real state of play is when it comes to your progress, your skills, your capabilities and your development.

2. A shared understanding of the difference between what's already been addressed and what remains to be achieved.

3. A definite sense of a relationship in which you can both handle the big stuff. Which makes it all the more likely that the next time the two of you need a big conversation, you'll get onto it earlier and handle it more confidently. Together.

Key thoughts

1. Initiate your own feedback conversation, don't wait for someone to do it for you. And, whichever side of it you're on, *Navigate* well to set up clearly what the purpose and the territory of it is.

2. Be honest. Say what's really happening from your point of view by *Disclosing* and *Describing* things as precisely and as personally as you can.

3. Look to improve the process of feedback. *Navigate* and extend the conversation so you can check in with how it was for both of you, every time you get it or give it. That way, next time it'll be easier, more relevant and more thorough.

Symptoms of success

I was once sitting in on a learning session at McKinsey's in London, where a well-known business guru asked the gathered young crowd what the best sign was of a company that would be successful in three years' time. A symptom, if you like, of future success. Many brilliant hands sprang up to answer the question posed. What was it? Good holidays? A strong sense of allegiance to the business? A good mix of experience and youth? A solid six months of share growth? Democratic wages? High wages? No. It was none of these. It was simply whether or not a group of people – *every* time they had finished something – would sit down together and look at what they had just done. And ask how it could be improved. In other words: a feedback conversation.

Chapter 15
Imagine this

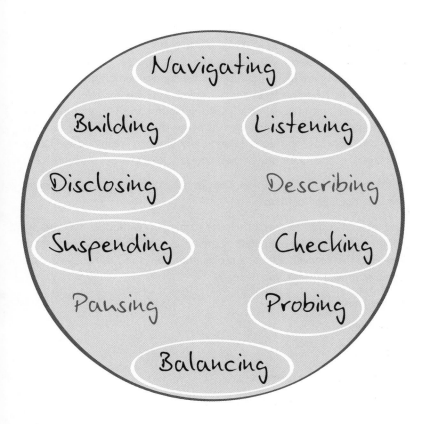

Let's talk creativity

A *say it and solve it* conversation isn't always significant because it tackles difficulties and problems. Sometimes – "solving it" means making the most of an opportunity, innovating or creating.

Anyone who's been part of any business, from a high-street shop to a global organisation, knows that growth and innovation go hand in hand. To stay ahead of the competition you need to do more than offer the same thing, week after week, month after month, year after year. A healthy business is as hungry to invent and imagine as it is capable of overcoming tough situations. And in the digital age, the mechanics of creativity are becoming democratised more and more as every day goes by. Much of what used to be farmed out to that special group of "creative" people can now be done in-house. Just think for a few moments about the small acts of creativity that used to be the domain of only specialists but now can be done in every workplace. Visuals for presentations, design of leaflets, images for advertising, sound and film editing, book publishing, website design... nearly every business in the world has someone who can, and does, take on any of these creative acts. (Quick hint if you're looking for one of these: they're usually under the age of 25.)

But these are acts of execution. They're the *expression* of creative ideas, not the generation of them.

And when it comes to the business of coming up with ideas, whether it's about selling, looking after staff or organising the Christmas party, there isn't, and there never will be, a replacement for good thinking. And for good, *creative* thinking, you need:

- imagination
- experience
- expertise
- knowledge of the business
- a desire to think beyond the obvious.

So you need your *senior* people (as well as the younger ones) to have creative conversations, because they'll have their own unique strengths to bring to bear.

(I'm sure young people come up with richer ideas when they're around older people. And vice versa.)

Ideas, please

One of the most *important* functions of conversation is to create new thoughts. New ways of serving the customer. New methods of getting stock from here to there, on time and in perfect condition. New channels through which you can let people know about what you do. It's the companies who think creatively, the business that stays at the sharpest edge of innovation, the organisation that looks for new opportunities, that gets to market first with a new application... these are the people who succeed and lead the way. And it's not enough to be creative once every few years. The internet has seen to it that the moment you have something new out there, others will follow, imitate and, sometimes, even trump your new offering. So, your ability to do new things in new ways is no longer an occasional necessity, it's a perennial requirement.

It's not hard to see, then, why creative thinking and fresh ideas are at a premium, more than ever before. Hence this chapter on how to have creative conversations that count. It's not a mysterious process. In fact, the same skills apply to this situation as any other. But some count more than others. So, as you read on, hold in your mind this thought: a conversation that counts is positive and focused on what *could* be, not what is. It's about creating new possibilities by thinking together.

Here are some quick ways to use nearly all of the 10 core conversation skills to that end.

Build, Navigate and Disclose

Building is essential when you want to create new ideas and solutions. Notice the germ of an idea and pick it up. Allow it to develop. Encourage it. Give it permission to flourish without judgement. Remember, the worst that can happen to an idea that's been built on is that it will reveal itself not to be a good one. In which case, you can move on confidently, but crucially, *without* that tension that can so easily develop when an idea is put forward and not given a chance.

So, let's start by just picking up a small idea and developing it. That little bit of construction might be all it takes to make something begin to sound credible:

> **"Your comment about changing working hours... Let's give it a couple of minutes to try it out. What if we let people choose their own hours? On three days a week, say..."**

Notice how by Navigating on the time front, you give permission to spend a short amount of time on Building something. And suddenly it's okay to talk about it for a while, because you've been explicit that you're not going to spend *too* much time on it.

Building is about adapting, too. You can take something that's general and make it crunchy or more specific:

> **"I'm wondering about your suggestion of making it a two-day event instead of three days. So – we'd halve everyone's time on their presentations. We shorten the lunch breaks. We finish half an hour later on both days. And everyone gets to go home on Thursday not Friday..."**

You can even add in a bit of Disclosing, if you think an idea is a bit on the wild side.

> **"Honestly? My instinct says this is never going to work but I don't want to write it off in case there's a stroke of genius in there. So, let's say we do reward everyone more often but with less. We assess sales quickly on a Friday morning. We announce it at lunchtime. And then give someone a bit of extra beer money that day?"**

Balance and Navigate

Creativity demands variety. Which is why Balancing is such a vital ingredient of a conversation that's looking to come up with new ideas. It takes you from one side of the spectrum to another. It creates surprises and almost guarantees the unpredictable. A bit like a long pass in a football match, switching the play from left to right, you suddenly find yourself in a position that offers new possibilities:

> **"Okay. So we've got some good thoughts around saving on costs. What about making money on this? We could make a small charge for something if it was good enough…"**

Again – to Balance well you have to notice where there's an imbalance. Acknowledge it. And then positively counter it:

> **"We've heard a lot now on how much new members of the team are bringing. I want to make sure we show the people who've been here for a long time that they are valued, too. Let's think about them for a while."**

You can see how Navigating is a natural partner in crime to Balancing.

Here's another example:

> **"Right, I count five or six examples there already of different ways people can recycle waste in the office. But it's at home where most of us unwrap the shopping, empty our dinner plates, wash our clothes. How about we spend roughly the same time as we just did on work-related ideas on ways of being greener at home? What we're trying to do is cut down on waste in general; it's not about keeping the office tidy!"**

Again – Navigating is the way to reassure people that, just because you're going to talk more, doesn't mean you're going to talk for its own sake. Sure – try different things out, but keep the conversation on course. That way your creativity energy and thinking will stay purposeful. Keep your eyes on the prize:

> **"It may well be that we'll come to a decision today on whether we have different coloured chairs or not. But let's not get distracted. For now let's stick to comfort and cost. Those are the two things we agreed would be most important to everyone, right?"**

It's worth remembering that Navigating has a rigour to it when it's done well. And creative conversations should contain plenty of rigour!

Listen, Check and Probe

Here's a group of likely lads; three skills that will breathe creativity into a conversation.

You can't put into practice *any* of the skills we've already talked about unless you've been Listening to other people. And the key secret with creative conversations is to Listen *for* the small things, only *just* peeking above the surface?

> "So – on the induction thing. When you were talking about your first day here, it sounded like you were a bit disappointed in the way you were first shown around the office... I wonder how many other people feel that way."

Or, indeed, what's *not* there as well as what is...

> "And there was something else. In your whole Description of that day, you didn't mention any of the leadership team..."

Even in slips of the tongue, accidental confusions, there can be great sources of creativity:

> "It was a mistake, I think, but you said 'official tour' rather than office tour..."

Listening for those small things means you might well unearth a little surprise here and there. And if you're alert enough to discover the unexpected, you're already on your way to coming up with more interesting ideas. So now you need to Check and Probe... to make sure that what you heard *was* what was meant!

> YOU:
>
> "It sounds like overall... we could have made that day a lot more special for you?"
>
> THEM:
>
> "Yes. It was partly a good thing, mind you. I was able to slip quietly into the team but... yes, my arrival didn't exactly feel like a particularly important thing for anyone else."

Checking often means a steady supply of valuable information coming your way. And it keeps you in touch with each other's ideas. So you can create something *together*, rather than two separate things.

Okay. Now you have some great territory into which you can Probe. Time to get under the surface now. In a merely efficient conversation, right now's where someone would write down: "Look into ways of making people feel special." In a *creative* conversation you Probe. There and then. And deeply.

More than once, if necessary:

> **"That's a terrible way for someone to think about their first day! What's that about? Are we *so* busy that we don't even think about things like that? There must be a reason why it doesn't even occur to us to mark someone's first day a bit more than that. I can't believe it's just busy diaries. Come on. Let's be really honest and get on the table some good reasons why we think we might let ourselves get away with that kind of thing..."**

Probing is incredibly important when you're looking for creative ideas or innovations. It's about asking the questions that go deeper, that reveal the purpose behind the product, the cause behind the commercial activity:

> **"Let's ask why we do this. Is it just to make money? If it was... would we be flogging ourselves so hard about quality? What is it that we really want to do to single ourselves out from the others? Let's ask ourselves that question. I know I'm sounding passionate. It's because this means a lot to me. But I mean it. Let's ask how we want to stand out from the rest. And then, and only then... let's decide what we want to do differently."**

(A bit of Navigating and Disclosing in there, too, for good measure.) But you can see, I hope, that Probing takes you into a different place. A deeper place. Where you can ask deeper questions. Which, in turn, will provoke and inspire deeper and better answers and ideas.

Key thoughts

1. *Build* and *Suspend* to give new, young ideas the best shot possible of coming to fruition.

2. Switch the conversation around to *Balance* the content and create unexpected ideas. *Navigate* as you go to make sure everyone buys into it.

3. *Listen* for the hidden gems. *Check* you're exploring fertile ground. And dig deep as you *Probe*.

Chapter 16
When yes isn't an option

Navigating

Building
Listening

Disclosing
Describing

Suspending
Checking

Pausing
Probing

Balancing

How to say no

There are times when the conversation you need *isn't* a creative one. In fact there are times when you barely need much of a conversation at all. Because, essentially, it's just about giving *bad* news. And bad news usually means there's a "No" in there somewhere.

You've lost the job. You didn't win the contract. The pay rise isn't going to happen. No flexible hours. No more money to spend.

Conversations like these are necessary; but they're hard and inherently negative. Because, inevitably, people are going to be upset or disappointed as a result. The best you can hope for, if you're on the receiving end of one of these, is that the conversation's fair and handled well. So, even if the news is bad, the delivery isn't.

Sadly, it's too often true that these are some of the worst handled conversations in the workplace. So, on top of the natural sense of disappointment at the outcome, the process is awkward or badly managed.

So, if it falls to you – as it's bound to at some point – to give someone some bad news, how you deal with the conversation could do a great deal to make it a less unpalatable and unhappy experience.

Depending on your nature, of course, it's possible to see an ending of one thing as the start of something else. It rarely feels like it at the time, but the "gift of goodbye" often can prompt new possibilities. There's at least a release in knowing, if little else. A release to think and talk about other things.

(Resist the temptation to be cynical. Some of my best beginnings have started as endings.)

So let's approach this differently. Let's look at what you can do to make a "No" conversation into something that's healthy, fair and authentic.

Time and Space and Navigate

This is a great example of a situation when it matters tremendously that a conversation feels safe and collective. Turning someone down, or telling them their pet project is being stopped in its tracks, will never be a moment to celebrate, but it can be a moment to take stock and look again.

First, let's do the right thing and make sure the conversation happens in the right Time and Space. Somewhere that's private and quiet, and at a time when it doesn't feel rushed or inconvenient. Don't overdo it. Content is king in this situation, but anything simple that shows you're considering the recipient of the oncoming bad news is a positive step in the right direction. A fresh glass of water. A box of tissues. That sort of thing.

Now, to help yourself be a good "guide" on this journey for whoever it is you're going to talk to, before you even get *near* the conversation itself, do some homework. Consider from *their* point of view how they might feel about the decision. What is it they'll be losing by hearing the word "No"? Will it be about status? Money? Their own development, perhaps? Is it something they've wanted to happen for a long time, or has the prospect of a new job or a bigger budget been raised only recently? Knowledge of these things again shows you care, long before you even step into the room. Has the possibility of good news been driving their actions recently? Have they delayed moving house? Have they held off on a decision about a child's school? Or put off booking a holiday? If anything like these examples is the case, they'll probably take it hard. So spend some time imagining what the implications might be for them and what it's going to feel like when you give them what is, essentially, a rejection. It's not a pleasant task, but your job in this position is to attend to these things. It's part of stepping out of the conversation even before it's begun.

And think of course, too, about what the positives *could* be from at least having the news clearly known and out there. These things, too, show that you've been thinking about them, which will go a long way.

When you finally reach the moment of the conversation, be explicit about the purpose of it and of your understanding of how significant it is for them. Swiftly and concisely let them know how it's going to work:

"Okay. Let's not waste any time. I'm sure you just want the news. So I'm going to let you know where things stand. And then, obviously, I'm here to answer any questions you might have."

Describe, Disclose, Pause and Balance

So, the inescapable moment is here. Don't try to avoid it. No small talk. No loose chat that could be interpreted as a good or bad signal. There is only one subject to talk about.

Give them the news.

And remember, Describing is about finding the best possible language for the individual involved, given the situation. Right now, that means giving them a nice clear headline up front. Give them the news.

> "So – we're not going to offer you the job."

There – the news is given. The worst is done. *Now* the most generous thing you can do is keep talking for a while and not ask anything of them. Partly to fill the space while they absorb the news. And partly to give them the background to the decision they deserve. Give them a full picture, but with no more detail than they need to know.

> "It was down to three people. You were right up there. But, after some really thorough consideration, we decided that right now you're still just a bit too inexperienced to take this role on. You gave a really good interview. But it's no."

You've been as good a Describer as you can be. You were clear, concise and accurate.

And now, time to Navigate again. And to make it the beginning of an actual conversation, which up until now hasn't really been possible, because you held all the cards. Now, you can begin to re-establish a Balance in what's been a one-way conversation...

> "We'd like you to know what we really liked about you in the interview. I think you might find it helpful. We can do that now or later. What's good for you?"

Just a bit of gentle Balancing and Navigating enables some equality to come back into the room. In one sense, it doesn't really matter what they say immediately. The point is that they're able to take part again in a conversation, rather than be on the receiving end of a monologue.

Don't be tempted, though, just to fill the air with words. Pausing might well be the best use of time here. Create some time to think. And give *permission* for it to happen:

> "I'm here to answer any questions you have. But if you just want to sit for a minute or two and think, that's totally fine. I'm happy to give you some time to think. I think it's important to have a few moments to gather your thoughts at moments like this."

Disclosing your own perspective is so much more personal and powerful than quoting others or generalising.

Empathy

And, finally, if you do get into a short debrief around why they didn't get the job, the contract or anything else, just a little bit of empathy will go a long way, especially with someone who's disappointed. So give them something positive to take away. Something that will mean something to them. Something that's meant for them. Find something positive about how that person was with you. And acknowledge it. Thank them for it. But make it particular to them.

You might remember from Chapter 3 the section on different strokes for different folks. If they are an audio person, acknowledge something they said and you heard. For example: tell them that they *sounded* like someone who knew what they were talking about and who was ready for a new challenge. If they're kinaesthetic, again talk to them in their language: tell them something they can *get hold of*. That their presence was a positive one in the room. If they're visual, you could say that they *look like* someone with a bright future ahead of them. This may sound simplistic – but right at the moment of disappointment, to have someone reach out and talk to you in *your* language will be of disproportionate value.

So...

Key thoughts

1. *Navigate* skilfully. Before you meet your interviewee, do your homework. When you meet, let them know how the opening of the conversation is going to go.

2. In the conversation itself, be honest enough to *Disclose* what you really think. *Describe* well by being concise, to the point and use examples. *Pause* well by giving time to reflect. And, once you've given bad news, restore *Balance* to the conversation by inviting them to influence the subsequent feedback session.

3. *Describe* positive things in *their* kind of language: visual, kinaesthetic or audio.

Chapter 17
We're all in this together

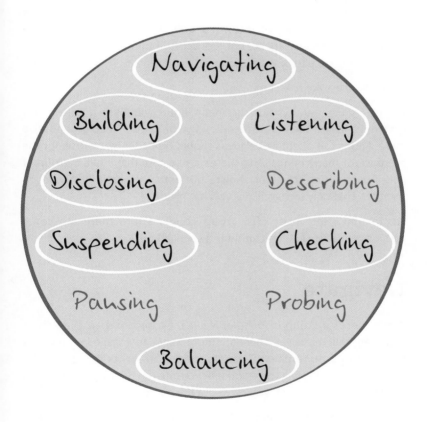

Making group conversations work

We instinctively think of a conversation as being between just two people. But, in fact, the reality is that at work most conversations happen in groups. Working groups, project teams, colleagues and clients, no matter who the people are, there are usually at least three or four of them.

Group conversations are essential to any good working practice. Even if, ultimately, there is one decision maker, a conversation that really matters should be doing a lot more than *just* making choices; it generates ideas and a shared sense of involvement and inclusion. Get people around a table, invent the ideas *with* them, and they become not just passengers but participants. They're informed and on board. They become advocates for the way ahead, not just because they're told about it but because they are part of the reasoning behind it.

Of course there are risks, too.

There's a danger always that too many inputs will dilute a pure idea. I have never heard the phrase "decision by committee" used as a positive thing. And yet, it ought to be. Ideas should be better, not worse, for the presence of many minds. And there's a risk, too, that while a group of people are sitting together, they're not actually *working* or *thinking* together. That only the familiar voices are heard.

So, to make the most of a group conversation, there are some particularly useful skills we can shine a spotlight on.

Navigate

When there's a group of people, Navigating becomes an even more important skill than ever. There are more minds to engage, more voices to encourage, more pairs of ears to tune in to what's being said. So, whoever it is that Navigates – and it needn't be the boss, by the way – it's critical that, at the outset, you carve out the purpose and parameters:

> **"So we're here to do several things. To build on the ideas we have so far, to make some decisions on budget and just to ask ourselves if we're missing anything obvious..."**

But this is just the basic, entry point of Navigating. The hygiene of the conversation, if you like. What about the health of it? A good Navigator will outline and make explicit the opportunities and dangers of a conversation:

> **"Now, we have as many points of view as we have people sitting around the table. And that difference is a strength, not a weakness. So, let's bring all points of view into the conversation. Negative voices and positive ones. If you have doubts, express them. If you think we're on course – say so. Plus, we need to cover a lot of territory in the 90 minutes we have. So let's be concise, straightforward and purposeful. Agreed?"**

It's the explicitness of Navigating that makes it such a powerful tool. Now you're set to reference this set of guidelines later, if you drift off course or if anyone speaks for too long. And at the end of a group conversation, you can Navigate again, lightly but directly:

> **"That was tough. But we did it. Thank you, everyone. We did what we said we'd do and that's quite an achievement, given how tough some of those topics were. We didn't fall out. It got a little bit tense at times, but that five-minute time-out in the middle seemed to sort that out. That was an inspired suggestion. I think everyone at some point helped shift things on. So. Well done. We've agreed to take action on four out of five things. And we'll pick up the hanging thread next week. Thanks. We're done."**

What have you achieved by adding this little post-script Navigation? Two very important things: first, you've recognised the role everyone played, which reminds every single person around the table that they've played their part, no matter how small. And, second, you've just made the next conversation a great deal easier, by reinforcing the fact that, even when things got tricky, they were safe.

Balance

If you Navigate well, you'll help yourself to Balance well. So enjoy getting a wide spread of views that will sustain and enrich the conversation. Consciously look for counter-views. Invite in the voice of caution to Balance the gung-ho attitude of the previous contributor.

But, bear in mind that just because there are many voices, it doesn't mean there's a full mix of perspectives. Get the group to do some of the work for you. Ask them to consider what someone outside might think.

"We're all over 30... What would your teenage son or daughter say if they were round this table now?"

Disclose

In a group conversation, another risk is that you or others will ameliorate or soften your point of view to make it easier to agree with. Not many people take pleasure in upsetting the apple cart. So the danger is – in order to keep the group together and form one shared opinion – individuals temper what they really think and feel. While this might come from a good place, what you end up with is a less radical, less spiky conversation. It'll count a little less because no one's saying what they're thinking.

This isn't necessary.

If you want the best conversation possible, it's as crucial as ever to Disclose, to put your background in the foreground. To say what you mean and mean what you say. It's not about politeness. It's about respect. So be sensitive – of course. Be appropriate – naturally. But don't be tempted to be dishonest. Instead, be as frank and candid as you dare. You'll help not just yourself, but everyone else, too. (Honesty in a group is like an infection that's good for you – it spreads.)

And if in doubt, remember to ask yourself the key question: "Is it helpful to the conversation right now for me to keep what I'm thinking to myself?" Yes or no. You decide. And, if you can't, go to the group:

"I want to know if I can really say what I'm thinking. Is it okay if I do that? Even if it's tough to hear..."

A good start. But what could be better? Share the struggle. Disclose about wanting to Disclose! Like this:

"I'm in a quandary here. I'm struggling as to how much to say. I want to help move things along. I want us to make a strong, clear

decision that helps everyone. It's that that's driving me to say what I'm thinking... Is it okay if I do that? Even if it's tough to hear...?"

Now you're in business. You've shared your intention. You've said *why* you want to say what you want to say. You've Disclosed really clearly. You've done your bit for the health of the conversation. The group can step in now. And, either you'll prompt some kind of revision of the whole conversation:

> **"You know what, I think many of us might be feeling the same way. It feels like there's a tension between being really honest and maintaining the status quo. Maybe we should revisit what our goal is here. Let's take a break for a few minutes and talk about it when we come back."**

Or you'll find your desire to Disclose isn't as stressful for others as it is for you and it's welcomed with open arms:

> **"Just say it. We've already said that this is the time for being authentic and radical. Speak your mind freely and without fear of judgement..."**

Either way, there's progress.

Because you trusted the truth.

And the conversation just got better.

Listen and Check

Even with only two people in a conversation, from time to time confusion is likely to occur. And the more people there are, the more chances there are to misinterpret what's been said. So Listen keenly and Check as much as you can in a group conversation. You'll be thanked for it. Even if it takes 30 seconds every now and again to make sure you understand what's been said, it'll save time in the long run. Listen for the small things. And, if you hear something that doesn't sound quite right... Check as soon as you can before it gets too hard.

(If you're struggling to understand something, you're unlikely to be the only one who feels that way.)

"So, from what I'm hearing, you seem to be saying that, ultimately, you want to bring all the businesses together? Physically? Is that right?"

Another quick motto for you here – there's no such thing as a stupid question. If you're not *sure* you understand, that's reason enough to Check if you do or don't!

And, of course, Listening is entirely crucial in a group conversation and a great Listener will always Listen *for* as well as *to*. So Listen *for* the smaller, quieter voices. Listen *for* the ideas that might be buried or only half expressed.

Suspend and Build

And, finally, keep an open mind always in a group conversation. There may be just one dissenting voice. One radical point being made. Don't ever dismiss these voices or assume you know what they're going to say. Suspend your judgement if you possibly can. Even if they're not spot on, there might well be something in there that's useful.

Remember that sometimes new and brilliant ideas come from quiet or modest voices. Pick up on a modest contribution. Nurture it. Build it. And give it the opportunity to grow.

Key thoughts

1. Make the best of the group by *Navigating* explicitly at the outset on what they can bring to the conversation.

2. Encourage as wide a range of authentic opinions as you can – by *Disclosing* and *Balancing* explicitly.

3. And keep an open mind. *Listen* for small, unusual things. *Suspend* your instinct to judge them. And help *Build* them, to see if they have potential to blossom into something of real value.

Chapter 18
Cancel
everything

Conversations in moments of crisis

"Think the unthinkable" is a hard instruction to follow. Why? Because it's a paradoxical idea. How can you possibly think up something that's impossible to imagine?

It's hard enough when it's a direction in good times. "Dream up something extraordinary!" we might be told. "Come up with something no one has ever thought of before!" It's tough. But not impossible.

Occasionally, though, it's harder than that. Sadly, thinking the unthinkable doesn't always come as such a positive call to arms.

A project is halfway through its course. But the cost has trebled in one year. Pull it.

A conference has been booked, invites have been sent, hotels have been paid for. The timing's wrong. Postpone it.

A job's been advertised, first-round interviews have happened. No one's up to the mark. Appoint no one.

Global team meetings are scheduled, holidays are booked around them. Budgets and holidays are cut. Freeze all global travel.

Sometimes things like this just have to happen. There are costs to these decisions. Some are obvious and immediate. Some are unexpected and won't appear until much further down the line. There are always risks associated with taking these kind of crisis-driven decisions. But when the risk of *not* taking those decisions is deemed too great, bold choices have to be made. And serious conversations need to be had.

Perhaps the greatest risk at moments of crisis is that the panic and fear that naturally associate themselves with bad news, infect the conversations that are required. Ironically, the last thing you need when you're frightened is a fearful conversation. It's at moments like this, when all bets are off, when the stakes are at their highest, when things are worse than anyone could possibly have imagined, when panic sets in, that you need, more than ever, a *say it and solve it* conversation.

So – how do we create the solid, reliable, calm conversation we need at moments of crisis?

Disclosing

First and foremost, when things are bad, one sure way to make them worse is to be dishonest. It's tempting, of course, to find some hope by massaging the truth. To make things appear to be a little less awful than they are. But, no matter how bad the crisis, what people *need* and want from a conversation at times like this is something they can *trust*. And trust comes from honesty. So, if you find yourself having to explain what's happening, be ruthless with yourself and others. Say clearly and honestly *only* what you know to be true. And be honest about what you don't.

Avoid the code, speculation and general reassurance you'd *like* to give:

> **"Yes, there's been an incident of some kind. An accident, I assume. I doubt anyone would have started a fire deliberately. Anyway. It's serious, of course it is, but let's keep our fingers crossed. Apparently there are a few injuries, but I'm sure everyone will be all right."**

(Don't confuse being nice with being helpful. No-one will thank you in the long run for pretending something's going to be okay when you know it's not.)

Instead, simply put out there what you *know* to be true:

> **"I don't know as much as I'd like to about what's happening. But what I do know is this: there's been a fire and it's a serious one. We have very little information so far. But it's clear that people have been hurt. So I'm preparing to hear more bad news, I'm afraid."**

Telling people that you're expecting to hear more bad news is honest. Telling *other* people to expect bad news is different. At times of crisis, stick to what's certain and what you're thinking, not what other people should think.

And remember, to help you be honest, say *why* you're being honest:

> **"Right, then. This isn't an easy meeting to start, but I want to be open with you. Honestly, I'd rather wait until everything was certain, but because I'm aware that rumours are flying around, I don't want you to be guessing what's true and what's not. So here's the toughest bit: it looks like we're going to be sold as a business."**

Navigate

Boy, do you need to Navigate in a crisis. There couldn't *be* a more important moment for holding onto the course of a conversation. When emotions are high, when people are worried or frightened, you need to keep a steady hand on the tiller.

Knowing what a conversation is and isn't about is crucial:

> **"So let's really focus on being as calm as we can. And let's be clear on what we're able to achieve, given what's happening. It seems to me that we need to go through all our individual lists of people that we've already invited, amalgamate those lists and then divide and conquer to get on to them as soon as we can and tell them it's cancelled. Let's not worry about what we say to them for now. We'll do that once we have one list to work from. Agreed?"**

And when emotions are running high – when the weather is volatile as it were – your Navigation has to be as flexible as it is clear:

> **"Okay, so it's clear that some people are finding the idea of making phone calls too upsetting. We can't afford to slow down, but maybe we need to try something else. How about we divide into two teams? One to do the calls, and another to keep gathering the information? That way we can reduce the number of people on the phone but keep up the pace at which we're contacting people. What do we think?"**

And, when people are wavering, it is a good time to remind them of the purpose of the conversation and how it needs to be:

> **"If people don't feel like contributing or talking, that's fine. Feel free just to Listen. This is one of those times, I think, when what's most**

important is that we're all in the same place in terms of what we know. Does that sound about right?"

Describe and Pause

When the stakes are really high and there's a sense of time being of the essence, it's more important than usual that you're economic with what you say. So speak concisely. *Really* consider how little, not how much, you need to speak. And allow yourself time to think of the best way to express yourself.

> "Right. Give me a few seconds to think for a moment... Okay. I think what I want to say is this: let's do what we have to do. We need to offer a full refund. To everyone. That's it for me. It's that simple."

Balance and Probe

When you're in crisis mode, often you need to think quickly *and* creatively. Balancing is an extremely valuable skill in situations that call for conversations like this. Crises tend to bring out the hurried thinker in us all, which can lead to making rash and rushed decisions. Balancing can give you a fast track to finding unusual solutions.

> "So, we have half the budget we had. All of our suggestions so far have been about incrementally reducing the number of people we have on the project, which is going to mean losing the expertise. What about thinking radically? If we were to keep the people and the expertise but halve the time of the whole event?"

When you need quick but big thinking, it's tempting to ask wide open questions like:

> "Have we got it covered from all sides?"

Or:

> "Does anyone have anything to add that might be useful?"

But when there's a fast-ticking clock, big open questions like that can sometimes create their own kind of ideas paralysis. So, if you want to Probe – to look for unusual solutions that might lie beneath the surface – try asking punchy, sharp, closed questions instead:

> **"What other budgets could help us out here? Have any departments underspent this year?"**

> **"Which of our partners are in the same boat as us and could use some cost cutting? Are any of them looking to run an event in the same month?"**

> **"What's most important here? That we get people together physically or that we have a single moment in time where we cascade the new strategy?"**

> **"Is there a virtual way of running this event? Have we ever looked at how much it would cost to bring together everyone in one global teleconference event?"**

Listen, Check and Suspend

Finally, there aren't many good things about a crisis. But there is one. People are often more likely to try out new things, perhaps because traditional methods have in some way been part of the problem that's created the crisis. So it's worthwhile Listening for small things that might be the beginning of a fresh idea. And, especially when you're having a significant conversation in a frenetic or panicky atmosphere – where it's tempting to rush into action without thinking things through – try to Suspend your instinct to judge too quickly in a conversation. It's counter-intuitive, of course, when things are moving fast, but a crisis is exactly the kind of moment when a conversation will count for more if you can resist the impulse to move swiftly at any cost. Just a small amount of interrogation might well improve or reveal an idea that's seriously going to help things.

The same thought applies to Checking, which might feel like the *last* thing you want to do when there's a crisis unravelling in front of you.

But it's a rare and invaluable skill in situations when you're looking for new thoughts quickly, because when you Check, even if someone's *suggestion* isn't necessarily the hole-in-one solution you need, there might be something in the thought that's hidden just behind it that gives you exactly what you need.

Let's say there's been a natural disaster in a region of the world that has affected your employees. You're meeting as part of a response team and this suggestion comes your way:

> **"I think we ought to reach out now. People are really worried about their jobs and the factory. We should let them know that we're there for them. Not to give them a quick solution, more to let them know we're aware of what's happening and it's important to us."**

If you Listen well, you'll find there's more to do than simply agree or disagree with this idea. And if you Suspend your instinct to immediately decide if this is a good idea or a bad one, you'll create space first to Check to make sure you understand the thinking and the intention, not just the words.

> **"So you're saying that people will want to know they're not alone? That we're thinking about them and trying to work out the best way to help them?"**

> **"Yes, totally. When I was there last year, I remember feeling shocked at how much they feel isolated from the central business anyway. They're not big stores. Some of the units are tiny internet cafés. This kind of incident will make it ten times worse for them."**

> **"So – let them know we're on their side? That we see it as something we're all involved with?"**

(Small acts of Checking like this can be done so quickly!)

> **"Not just that. Let's show them we're doing something concrete. That we're working on their behalf."**

The idea is being defined and refined in front of you. Checking often leads to a honing or sharpening of an idea.

Now, your instinct to judge might have leapt into view at the words: "show them we're working on their behalf". Something like this will tempt you to have an opinion on it. Either to agree or disagree with it. Resist both. Suspend your decision to think of it as a risky venture or an exciting opportunity to do something positive. Just keep an open mind. And use your Listening skills. Listen for small things...

> **"You were out there last year? Is there anyone you know who you could talk to? If we could run any ideas past someone out there on the ground, that might be a big help... Maybe we can help get the internet back up using a satellite feed or something?"**

And so an idea is born.

Key thoughts

1. When things are in crisis, *Disclose* whatever you can, but only what *you know* to be true or else you risk adding to uncertainty.

2. *Navigating* is crucial when people are anxious and panicking. Stay focused on clarity of purpose. You don't need to have answers; keeping things calm is a hugely useful contribution to a conversation that needs to create swift, but thoughtful, action.

3. *Check*, *Listen* and *Suspend*, even though the clock is ticking. You might unearth new and unexpected ideas by resisting the urge to make hasty, binary decisions based on on the first things you hear.

Chapter 19
That special
someone

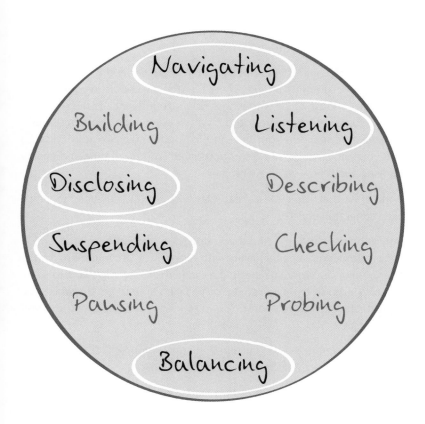

Dealing with your boss

Most of us have a boss. In one form or another.

Actually, there's no such thing as *a* boss. There's only *your* boss. And they're as much of an individual as you are. So, not all of this chapter might be about *your* boss. But some of it might be.

What's in a boss?

If you think about it, whatever the context, there's one critical factor that makes the relationship between you and your boss a distinctive one. He or she has a position, and therefore a status, that's granted to them by someone *other* than you.

They were chosen *for* you, not by you. And it's partly *this* dynamic that makes the relationship unique. There aren't many people in your life that you didn't choose to be with whose role is to influence your behaviour and the way you spend your time. Which is why your boss occupies a very specific space in your life. And, consequently, why it's natural to find yourself carving out a disproportionate amount of time and energy thinking about how you are with them.

It might be that you have a great relationship with your boss. In which case, congratulations!

But, perhaps you don't. And if you don't, I'm prepared to bet there's a conversation you imagine having with him or her. On your own. On the train home from work, maybe. In the car. In the shower. Walking to work. You may even have rehearsed it. You've taken time to get the words *just* right to start it. You've edited. You've refined it. Several times. But you haven't *had* it.

Because, ultimately, you end up thinking to yourself: "I could never actually *say* those things to *them*." But could you?

Could you (yes *you*, not him or her) maybe even improve the way things are between you and your boss, simply by adjusting the way you talk and Listen to them? Let's consider that.

Break the rules

When it comes to having conversations that count with your boss, it sometimes feels like there's a set of rules that creates problems for you. Rules like:

1. You can't say what you really think (because they might not agree).

2. You need to give them a version of events they'll like (rather than tell them what's actually happening).

3. It's important to distance yourself from everything (in case they don't like it and you get into trouble).

These are commonly held, but often unspoken, rules. They're based on fear. And they're not helpful. But, for many people, they're very real.

I'd like to respectfully suggest something.

Break these rules. And instead, try employing some of the skills we've talked about here. If you're doubting whether it will work, think about the potential rewards for a few moments.

- You'll save yourself time, tension and wasted energy.

- You'll find working with your boss feels like working *with* your boss not *against* him or her.

- The choices and decisions you make together will start happening more quickly and more thoughtfully.

- The outcomes will be better and more mutually satisfying.

- Your relationship will improve.

- You may even find that he or she starts to reward and applaud you for being someone who's not afraid to broach the big conversations.

(Life's too short to carry around resentments. So have the conversation you need to have. And reap the rewards.)

So what then, are the particular things you should do more of to create a better relationship with this special person? Which skills are especially important when it comes to dealing with your boss?

Suspend and Listen

First, you might need to clear away some preconceptions about your boss. That perhaps they don't care. That they're too busy. That they won't hear anything you say or act on anything you suggest. That they don't remember anything you say. That they're too preoccupied with something else. If you believe these things, all you'll do is amplify any frustrations you have and raise the bar of any obstacles in your own path. So start with an open mind. And reclaim an adult-to-adult relationship between you. Treat your boss as a grown up. As a fellow human being. As an equal. Listen to them with fresh ears. As if you've not heard them speak before. Listen for clues. For what's behind the words. You'll be surprised what a difference it can make if you Suspend what you think to be true.

Whatever your history with your boss, you're both people who get up in the morning and try to make stuff happen. So decide to make something happen together. Level the ground between you. Respect the individual, not the job title. Forget the meeting room. And make room to meet the person not the job title.

Now, you're ready to start *really* preparing for that conversation.

Balance

You. And your boss. Of course, in the most fundamental sense, you're two equal human beings. But in a work context there's an inherent difference in status between you. Of course there is. You'll both walk into the room with that difference clearly understood and you'll walk *out* of the room the same way. They'll still be your boss. You'll still be working *for* them (and not vice versa). But be careful that this imbalance doesn't get into the grain of an important conversation between you. If you want to have a conversation that counts, if you truly want to solve the problem in front of you and sort things out for good, then a significant difference of status tends not to be helpful. So Balance things at the beginning of a conversation, by finding an equal weight in the conversation. It's in both your interests to dissolve any sense of inequality:

> **"I'm conscious that you have a great deal more experience than me. But in terms of what I can offer, I do have a relatively fresh pair of eyes. Perhaps I can offer something valuable by looking at this more objectively?"**

Of course, at some point, if there's a clean decision to be made, it'll be down to your boss to make the final call. That's as it should be. But *within* and during the conversation, you should both seek to find a way for you to input more or less equally.

Which brings us to the crucial area of how you manage that conversation…

Navigate (Part 1)

What's *so* useful about Navigating in the context of a conversation with your boss is that it draws out – maybe it even insists on – your capacity to work *together*. When the responsibility for how well a conversation goes is *shared*, when it's co-owned at the outset, you give yourselves a fighting chance of co-creating an outcome. So, if you consciously set up a strong sense of "we" in the conversation, you're more likely to get somewhere useful together and to gain something positive. It's not hard.

You can start with something as simple as the amount of time you're going to spend talking:

> **"How are we for time? We have until 3 pm, yes? We're in the same meeting then, too. Let's aim for 2.45 pm? Then we'll have time to prepare for the session with the finance team? I'm sure we could both do with a short break before then. How's that for you?"**

Not a seismic conversation exactly? It doesn't need to be. What it is, is a good start to a joint endeavour. Investing less than a minute into creating *a* sense of a *shared* project and an explicit commitment to collaborating. And then you can take it a stage further:

> **"Now – we have an agenda, I know, but this is one of those situations where, if we're not careful, we could skate over everything too lightly or get too deep into detail and not cover everything we need to. I'm happy to play the role of 'time police' if it'll help things flow..."**

You've opened the door. If your boss replies with something like this, then it's all systems go:

> **"Thanks. That'll help a lot. And why not give us a two-minute heads up when we're running out of time on each topic? Does that sound helpful?"**

If this happens – great. You know what the parameters are.

But, even if you get something more like this in response:

> **"No... I need you to be focused on content not time management. Let's just keep an eye on the clock collectively..."**

... there's a different point of view, which you can take on, of course. But don't do it silently and privately. *Keep* Navigating explicitly. Because the point of Navigating isn't to agree, it's to come *to an agreement* on a way of working for the conversation. To openly lock in together on how you're going to proceed:

> **"Okay. I'll monitor myself a bit more than usual. If you want me to take the gloves off... you say so. We'll work it out between us."**

> **"Exactly."**

Now you both know how things are going to be. No more guessing required. And you can get on with it.

Navigate (Part 2)

The other useful aspect to Navigating is that it "outs", or makes explicit, the *purpose* of the conversation. And, to get the journey of a conversation off to a good start, you need to make sure you're heading in the same direction. So get out onto the table first *why* you're having the conversation and then *what* the conversation should (and shouldn't) be about.

It's important to emphasise that you should be as *explicit* and *specific* as you possibly can be here. The more clearly you identify and create *together* a shared purpose for talking to each other, the more you can depend on it to help you as things progress. So when things get a bit wobbly – and in a conversation when the stakes are high they may well get wobbly – you can both reach confidently for that initial agreement as a solid handrail to keep things steady.

Let me give you an example.

Let's say you're a few minutes into a conversation with your boss. Things are getting harder. It feels like you're both going a bit off-course and you notice yourself hesitating around how honest to be. This is the moment when either of you can step out to Navigate briefly and say:

> **"We agreed, didn't we, that the reason for having this conversation was to *really* bottom things out and make some decisions. Not to avoid the tough stuff. Well, here we are dealing with the tough stuff. It feels like it's getting personal, which is fine. But I have some things that aren't all that easy to say and they might be hard to hear. So, I'm... getting less sure about how much I should say. But we agreed, didn't we, that we'd talk about whatever needed talking about. That the priority was to make these decisions. So I'm going to trust in that agreement. Okay?"**

It doesn't mean what you're about to say will be easy, but it does mean you'll be able to say it. And all you've done is step out of the content temporarily and ask for some reassurance that you can abide by the guidelines you co-created at the outset; in this case, that it's okay to be honest throughout, despite the natural obstructions and feelings of awkwardness that have come along.

So, there are many ways to improve the course of a conversation with your boss and we'll touch lightly on some more now. But if you can make Navigating a priority early on, you'll be well set up for what follows.

Disclose

So you've done the groundwork by Navigating and created together the optimum conditions for honesty. But still, when it comes to *that moment* in a conversation when you want to be really honest – there's still a moment of threshold. You're still wondering whether or not to say the *actual thing* that's in your head when so much is at stake.

So, ask the question that'll make it so much easier to know the answer:

> **"If I say what I'm thinking, is it going to help the conversation?"**

If the answer is yes, then make the call. Make the choice. And speak!

Remember from the chapter on Disclosing – to first say *why* you want to be honest:

> **"This is important to me. More than money, hours or anything else. So I need to know I'm working on a project that's ethical. I can't stay here if I don't know that we're thoroughly ethical. So I have to push you, I'm afraid. Are we hiding anything about the sourcing of our materials?"**

Or, more personally:

> **"I don't want to make up stories about where I am when I'm not in the office, so I've talked to my husband and we feel we ought to include you on this. I'm pregnant. I've lost a baby before now so we're not telling anyone else. I hope you can keep it just between us for now."**

So. There's a lot of content in there. And, to be honest, there could be a lot more. Any working relationship can be a complex one. But the one with your boss is unique. We may have scratched only the surface. But let's summarise briefly what we've talked about here.

Key thoughts

1. Make the decision to talk with and *Listen* to your Boss with an open mind. *Suspend* what you think you know about them. And reclaim the *Balance* in status between you, if only for the duration of the conversation.

2. Work *with* your boss, not against him or her. Give yourself the best chance of co-creating a positive outcome to a conversation, by *Navigating* well at the start. Make sure you find out *why* you're both having the conversation. A shared motivation is an enriched fuel that will take you further.

3. If it serves the conversation, be bold enough to *Disclose*. First say why you need to be honest. And then, be honest.

I look up to him

I once coached a senior executive for a few years on and off. A man who was – it seemed to me, anyway – at the very top of a business. He was the classic picture of a modern, successful man. He had charisma, certainty, curiosity and he relished being the boss. Not because he had control, but actually, because he could serve. He was, in that sense, a traditional man. I enjoyed our sessions together, working as we did on big speeches, set pieces and moments of impact. And then, one day, he turned up for a working session, almost unrecognisable. Stressed. Weighed down. Frustrated. Volatile. Angry, even. And hopeless to work with. So we stopped. And talked. I Listened. It took a while, but eventually I discovered what had happened. I found out that what was causing this irrational, upsetting, difficult behaviour was not something he'd done. But a line had been crossed. Someone else, not him, had decided that some of the people who worked for him were to suffer the consequences of a clumsy, thoughtless piece of management. How could that possibly happen, I wondered naively? Surely, you're the boss. If you don't agree, it doesn't have to happen. I was wrong. And what I discovered is worth remembering when your boss behaves badly. My boss, it turned out, had a boss. Most of them do.

Chapter 20
The customer is king (or queen)

Conversation as great service

Customer service comes in all shapes and sizes. Whether your workplace is a restaurant or a global food supplier, you have customers. And the quality of service you give those customers will make or break you as a business. Of course, much of what you provide for your customers is about efficiency. Is the food hot? Are the shelves full? Did you deliver on time? These are the physical properties of good customer service.

But, beyond these "hard" deliverables, what makes the difference to us as consumers or customers is a recognition that we're individual people with individual needs. And in a world where differentiation is increasingly minuscule in terms of hardware and logistics, what makes a difference now is the personal touch.

And conversation sits right at the heart of customer service. The way in which we're dealt with – the way in which we're spoken to by the people providing a service to us is important to us. Our "customer experience" is increasingly what distinguishes one provider from another.

On the receiving end, we're quick to acknowledge the importance of a good conversation. It's not only the interest rate that influences how we feel about staying with our bank, it's how our accounts manager deals with our query about the £30 charge for a temporary overdraft we incurred last month. If a sultry teenage waiter grumpily drops a plate onto the table, while he mumbles and fumbles indistinctly, it doesn't matter how good the food is, your experience isn't a happy one. And, in the same way that an approachable, friendly air hostess can make you feel good about yourself, even on a delayed and bumpy flight, a disembodied screen-reading telephone customer advisor can spoil our lunchtime, even if we manage successfully to get the correction made on a wayward phone bill.

So, now, let's think about how you deal with *your* customers and how the quality of the conversations you have with them counts for an awful lot. Which of the conversation skills make a *real* difference in this area?

Navigate and Describe

Looking after the conversation is a great way to look after your customer. So Navigating skilfully will help you to keep them close to you on the journey of the conversation. And if you can Describe things richly but concisely, your customer will find you easier and more engaging to talk with.

Let's start with Navigating. Being clear about what you want to achieve at the beginning of a conversation – sharing your intention – is a sure sign that you care how well it goes. And it's especially important when things have gone wrong. When there's been a bump in the road and you need to repair things, be clear about the *purpose* of the conversation:

> **"I want to explain *exactly* what's been happening so you at least know what's going on. Then we can choose what the best plan of action is from there. Yes?"**

That last little word is crucial. You're offering a gentle contract and asking: "Are we in this together?" When someone's experienced poor service they feel the opposite of togetherness. They feel isolated and abandoned. They feel – literally – on the other side of you. So you're dealing with someone who at best feels a bit defensive. At worst, they feel like an enemy. So your priority is to befriend them again and get them back on the shared journey towards solving the situation.

You need to regain their trust and confidence. And part of that process is about clearing away confusion. So being *clear* is critical, which is why how well you Describe things is important when you're building bridges with a customer.

Get to the point. Don't waffle. Be specific, clear *and* complete. Offer the customer a full picture of the *context*, not just the content, and they'll be able to see what's happening. It's down to you to shed light on proceedings so they won't have that horrible feeling of being in the dark.

So, let's start with a nice practical example. You're a waiter and you need to explain why things are delayed.

> **"I'm so sorry. The chef's had a difficult afternoon."**

This is not a good start.

I suppose you could say it's clear. But it's not anything like complete. (And it's pretty useless to the poor customer, who might *also* have had a difficult afternoon.)

So, give some more detail. Good Describing is about being specific:

> **"I'm so sorry. The chef had to deal with a party of 16 people who turned up without booking about 90 minutes ago. We've got their mains sorted so we can focus on our regular customers now."**

Or let's look at an example of talking to a customer on a much larger scale, giving a full and clear picture of what's caused the problem:

> **"I'm afraid your delivery's not going to be there today. We were told at 6 am this morning that the snowstorms in Poland have delayed deliveries much more seriously than we'd hoped. I'm so sorry. We have emergency plans in place that mean in 48 hours we'll be back where we should be."**

It's hard to admit. But it's good because it's definite, it's detailed and it's direct. And it's still concise.

But great customer service, like a great conversation, isn't something you do *to* or *at* people. You do it *with* them.

It's tempting, when things go wrong, to retreat into a servant–master relationship; to blindly and generally assure your customer that "everything will be okay" soon. But, ultimately, this is a disrespectful way of dealing with customers.

We've all had builders who are working on two projects at the same time when they've told us we're their only client. And we know how galling it feels to have the wool pulled over our eyes. Don't be tempted to promise everyone everything and sneak around trying to patch things up behind the scenes. Navigate the journey side by side and make it a collaborative effort. It's the difference between an *us* thing and a *you against me* thing:

So, on a practical level:

1. Offer the customer the chance to make choices *with* you.

2. Change your language and use the word *we*.

3. Offer up alternative ways of moving from where you are to where you want to be.

> **"What can we do to help you most? I can give you a concise version, or a longer version..."**

> **"What's going to work for you? We can get you an alternative meal within 10 minutes, or I can hurry things along as best I can with your original order."**

> **"What I can do for you is call you every hour to let you know how close the delivery is, or I can put you in touch with someone who might have stock in the UK."**

The decisions are there to make together. This is a different approach to inventing the "perfect" solution and throwing it at your customer. You're *engaging* with them. You're *including* them. You're maintaining the relationship, by maintaining the conversation.

Find a solution together and your customer will recognise that, as well as wanting to solve the problem, you want to maintain a good, healthy, authentic relationship.

Disclose

An unhappy customer is much more forgiving if they know they're dealing with a real human being. Again, we know this from being the customer. It's when you know that Omar, Brian or Janice on the end of the phone takes a genuine interest in *your* situation and takes personal responsibility for it that you start to feel you're being cared about. So, if there's difficult news to impart, be bold enough to come clean. Admit it if something's gone wrong.

Invite your customer into a "secret" place of honesty, where they'll trust you and give you the time you need to resolve a problem:

> **"Can I be really straight with you?"**

Who's going to say no to that?

> **"Thank you. I appreciate that."**

(It might seem trivial, but saying thank you to something like this is an important use of Navigating. It seals the deal. They've accepted your explicit request to have a genuine, frank exchange, as one person to another, rather than tolerate the smoke and mirrors we tend to get when things go wrong.)

> **"Honestly? Monday's normally a much quieter evening than this. But we were caught totally off guard by a big party that arrived at 6 pm. So we're not anywhere near where we'd want to be in terms of waiting time. I'm sorry. Now... Between you and me, if you want to make that movie for 8 pm, there are only two dishes I'd recommend, to be sure you can leave in time."**

Honesty really is the best policy. The choice of items on the menu has gone down. But the quality of your relationship with the customer, and therefore the quality of their experience, has gone up.

Here's another good example of Navigating in order to Disclose and Describe, where you first *acknowledge* the reality of the situation and then offer a creative way forward. The language is simple, specific and clear. And your intention is out there to see:

> **"You're clearly in a hurry. Now, we could get into a detailed conversation about whether we can get you what you need by when you need it. But I don't want to add to your frustration and it feels to me like we might just waste your time when you need to make a quick decision. So, why don't I just level with you? This is unusual, I admit, but... I can have your starter ready in five minutes. And I can have your main course piping hot and ready for you immediately *after* the film? How does that sound? Great idea? Terrible idea?"**

It's a risk, sure. But you're going out of your way to think creatively. And, by being clear, complete and keeping the conversation "safe" in the sense that it's honest and (frankly) free of bullshit, you're doing something *much* more important than clinging on to a single order, that may not even make it on time.

You're putting the customer's needs first and, consequently, looking after the relationship.

Clear, honest, well-handled conversations strengthen the bond with a customer far more than apologetic servant/master relationships and form a huge part of great customer service.

(I was once taught that when you're late, the only really honest thing to say is: "I'm sorry. I didn't leave enough time to get here." Never mind the circumstances. It's always true.)

Now, let's look at a couple of other key skills when it comes to putting the customer first.

Listen, Suspend and Check

It's tempting to hear only what we *want* to hear from customers. In the same way that sometimes it's tempting to give them what we *have* rather than what they *need*.

But if we're to genuinely Listen to customers, it has to be with an open mind, Suspending our own wishes and judgements. Then, and only then, might we begin to hear the small things. The things that matter to the customer. If we really tune in. Picking up on the things that are perhaps only hinted at. And hearing what's *not* said as well as what *is*. *That's* good Listening.

So let's imagine you have a long-term regular customer in for a chat about how you could improve the way you work with them.

What might you notice, if a customer said something like this?

> **"From our point of view, one thing we'd appreciate is earlier notice about new innovations.**
>
> **It sometimes feels like we're only told about things that have been fully tested and piloted elsewhere. There's a good side to that, of course. It means a new system usually works. But we'll end up adapting it one way or the other, so maybe we should**

work together when it's being designed. We have ideas we could usefully offer, I think. We're not a big business in the way that you are so we can't create a huge programme of investment like you can. And our budget for innovation is a small one, relatively speaking. But I suppose it's all part of being thought of as more than just another customer."

Now, it's tempting, of course it is, to rush in with: "Yes, yes – that's a brilliant idea!" Don't!

First show you want to really get it by Checking that you've understood what they've said, by lightly summarising what you've heard.

A decent Check in this instance might be something as simple as this:

"So – you're saying we could involve you earlier, consult you on new processes and systems. Build ideas *with* you?"

That's not a bad summary. And the useful thing about Checking, remember, is that it works whatever the outcome. If you get it right, you'll encourage them to say a little more:

"Yes. Involve us more. Include us in the thinking not just the execution. There's some real expertise in our midst that I'm not even sure you know about..."

And, if you get it wrong, Checking is still a good idea. Because they get to adjust what you heard:

"Well, no – it's not just about involving us earlier. It's more about how you see us. How you view our relationship. It sometimes feels like we could work much more creatively together if you just saw us as partners rather than customers."

Just a simple Check can yield great things. It's not hard to do. But it's a great skill to use when you want to stay close to what a customer is really trying to get across to you.

By the way – did you notice that little hidden gem earlier?

Did you spot that small, but significant, clue to the treasure? In amongst all the content about working more closely, they said:

"... a huge programme of investment like you can. Our budget for innovation is a small one, relatively speaking."

They have a budget. For innovation.

It was briefly alluded to. But that's a significant thing. Which you could easily miss, unless you tune in and Listen really well. The benefits of Listening to your customer are many and mighty. Sometimes those benefits will be hard, fast and financial. Better tips. Better rates. Better deals. But the gold in them thar' hills won't be anything to do with money. You'll get information. Insight. And resources. All valuable and important rewards, well worth a bit of extra effort when it comes to Listening.

Probe

So, when we Listen to customers, we can do it much better if we simply "switch on". It's not a shock to you, I'm sure, to say that most consumer research in the world is data driven. But there are some things you can hear only if you have a *real* conversation with people. The change in tone as they move from trust to suspicion. The shift in energy or pace in the way people talk or the unexpected emphasis on a particular word. All these things can be heard only if you're there, Listening to them. Listening for clues, in a way that you can't, if all you have in front of you are collated facts and figures.

You can learn so much from the richness of conversation. And written questions are great tools but they'll tell us only half the story. To ask good questions, i.e. Probing questions, you need to be *there* to sense, as well as hear, the answers:

"So tell me why you *really* feel like that about it."

"What is it that gives you that shiver you mentioned?"

"When you say beautiful... what do you mean?"

There are questions that can come only if you've been there and heard the previous answer.

Key thoughts

1. *Disclose* to be honest with your customers. They'll respect you more.

2. *Navigate* to work out better solutions to problems *with* them, not for them.

3. *Listen* to them, and *Suspend* with an open mind.

Here to serve

There are no answers, just better questions. That's what my Mum said to me. And I think she's right. So, ask yourself some better questions, about the conversations you have with your customers. How much time does your business buy for research groups with people every year? Is it money well spent? What's the *quality* of those conversations? How about you get some customers in front of you? Don't pay someone else to do it. *You* do it. Try having a conversation of real quality with them. My bet is that there's not a business in the world (including mine) that wouldn't benefit from having more and crucially *better* conversations, face to face with their customers. So, if you're really interested in great customer service, sit down with some of them soon. And give them a damn good Listening to.

Chapter 21
Next slide,
please

Presenting yourself

Presentations have become a core part of working life in recent years.

We reach now for our laptops and the PowerPoint deck (or, if you're lucky, a more smoothly animated Keynote file) on a weekly, if not a daily basis for briefings, pitches, cascades and any number of smaller meetings.

Sadly, while the format may have become ubiquitous and the software has improved, many of the presentations are still an over-long, dreary procession of facts and charts. At best, they're a slideshow of images with headlines attached. At worst, they are a series of notes for speakers displayed on the screen with a list of bullet points and imported clip-art clichés. It's a rare thing to hear or see a presentation that's as compelling or as useful as it could be. Which is a great pity, because it's not difficult to improve the quality of a presentation.

And one of the ways in which you can improve your next presentation is to change something fundamental about it.

Not many people think of a presentation as a conversation. But it is.

(It's just a conversation in which your audience doesn't say very much.)

The most compelling presentations I've seen create or contain many of the skills of conversation that we've looked at here: Listening, Navigation, Description, Pausing, Balancing, Probing, Checking, Suspending, Building and Disclosing.

So, as a final chapter, let's identify how and why an awareness of these skills can make presentations far more interesting *and* effective.

Describe

A great presentation is a good deal about storytelling. And a core storytelling skill is Describing things in a powerful, compelling way.

You can capture the attention of an audience so easily by working your use of language harder.

So keep your sentences short and punchy.

Up the ante on your verbs (next time you want to "take the opportunity" try "seizing the day" instead).

Appeal to all three channels of learning:

- Give the *visual* people something to enjoy looking at.

- Give the *audio* people some sound-based words and phrases: "It was a time for hope. You could hear it in the way people talked to each other."

- And give the more *kinaesthetic* people something to *do*, even if it's as simple as putting their hands up if they agree or disagree with something. And talk in terms that will *touch* them; use the language of movement, heat, friction and expansion.

Navigate

An audience responds to being engaged with, not talked at. So think about your job more as a guide through the *journey* of a presentation as opposed to someone who's standing up telling people lots of things.

Here are four tactical ways of doing that:

1. First, let the audience in on what you're trying to achieve. Share your purpose, by answering the question: why am I here?

> **"What I'd like to do in the next 30 minutes is give you a different lens on what's happening for us as a business right now and the chance to consider why we might be in the situation we are. Because I think it might prompt some new ideas. And, at the end, I'd like to move to more of a dialogue, or at least a decent Q & A session."**

2. Now, give us an idea of the journey ahead. And equip us for that journey. Give us a role to play. A hat to wear, if you like. Give us the "rules". And tell us how you'd like us to behave as we move with you:

> **"For the next half an hour, I'd like you to think of yourselves not as diligent, efficient, responsible adults, but as playful coconspirators. And imagine that, actually, what we're doing is infecting people with optimism. That's our day job. Keep that in mind... as you Listen. And, please – interrupt me whenever you want to."**

3. And, at the end, close the loop for us. Acknowledge what kind of journey we've been on and bring us back to a more familiar perspective we recognise:

> **"So there we are. Thanks for making the effort to imagine with me how different things could be if we used our imagination. That was – I suppose – an exercise. But it was purposeful. And serious. I wanted you to experience something like the hope I felt when I first reconsidered what our business could be if we thought of ourselves differently. I'd be very interested to know what questions you have in your mind. Let's spend 10 minutes now building whatever thoughts you have into some ideas. Some things we could start doing today."**

4. Finally, as a good guide should, step out of the content occasionally and don't be afraid to include your audience on the shape and structure of your story.

> **"Let me take two minutes now to go into some detail on that particular point, then we'll come back to the big question..."**

> **"But, rather than give you too many facts and figures, I want to slow down a bit, and reach out to your hearts for a moment."**

Or:

> **"What we're looking at now, this is the *hinge* point of the whole strategy; the fulcrum of the story I want to share with you."**

These kinds of guiding comments give your audience a richer experience: context as well as content. And, by keeping them in touch with how far through the journey you are, they have a sense of being on the journey *with* you; and an idea of what responsibilities they have as participants, not passengers:

> "Okay, so we're about halfway through now. Thanks for being such attentive Listeners so far. Change of gear now and everything from here on is 100 per cent confidential. Are we okay with that?"

Check and Probe

When do you get to Check you've understood in a presentation? Surely you're doing the talking – so it should be your audience that's Checking?

Well – no. Twice, no.

First, precisely *because* you're doing the talking – and it's hard to involve everyone literally in a conversation while you're presenting – you have to take on *their* role. You need to Check *yourself*, for them. Asking yourself questions as you go through a presentation is a brilliant technique when you want to create the feel of a conversation. Like this:

> "So we wanted to double our growth? Now – that meant doubling our size, right? Well, actually, no. It meant doubling our market share."

If you Check *yourself* with a question, it gives a compelling sense of a dialogue; a story told in the present tense, rather than just a sequence of what happened next. And it opens up the chance for you to *respond*, not just to report:

> "So, there we were at a crossroads, if you like. So, in essence, was it a natural time for us to reflect and be bold about our ambitions? Well... yes and no. Actually, it felt like a natural moment to look forward, but oddly we didn't look back. And that might have been our mistake..."

And, of course, you can Probe in the same way, to create a more energised way of telling the story.

> "But, why? Why would we choose to make this decision now?"

"So, what lay behind this choice? Never mind what we told the press, what was *really* going on?"

And, finally, of course, when you take questions from the audience – and you should *always* take questions from the audience – to make sure you're responding to *their* enquiry, not your agenda, you need to make sure you understand what their question is, before you reply to it.

"Okay. So, if I understand you correctly, you're asking was it a choice we only made because we had to?"

"All right – let me see if I have this right, your question is: while this was clearly a response to the downturn, would we have made the same choice in good times? Is that right?"

It takes less than 10 seconds to Check you've understood a question and it's a great way of giving the audience a real sense that you're there for *them,* not just to serve your own purposes. It makes them feel, dare I say it, like they're having a conversation with you, rather than being on the receiving end of a speech!

And, when you do get a question, Probe in order to dig deeper and find out more about the question before you start to give an answer:

"What's the nature of your interest, I wonder?"

Listen

It's instinctive to go into "broadcast" mode when we're put on a stage and asked to present. So, one of the first casualties of that is often our capacity to receive or Listen. But, if you can present *and* Listen well to your audience, you'll be able to create a much more interesting dynamic in the room.

So keep your ears and eyes open throughout, tune in to their movements and sounds. And, if you can Listen, you'll find yourself able to say things like:

"Oh! That sounded like a little rustle of approval there..."

"I see there are a few nodding heads of recognition... that's interesting."

"That smile in the front row tells me I'm not the only person who's been optimistic with a budget recently..."

These are great ways to keep connected with the audience and to recognise their response to what you're saying. And by showing that you're Listening as well as talking, you're creating a healthy sense of conversation in the room.

And again, when you do take questions, make sure you Listen openly for *small things,* so you hear more than just the words from the audience. If you notice something about the way that something's said, you'll create a bond with the audience and it'll put you in a position to respond personally and not generally:

"It sounds like you know what you're talking about... do you have first-hand experience of this, I wonder?"

"By the way, your face lit up when you said the word 'sustainability'. I suspect you have a vested interest... Am I right?"

Disclose

And, finally, be honest.

As in any conversation that counts, when it comes to making a presentation, there is nothing duller than a rehearsed, fenced-off set of overly prepared statements. And there is nothing more *exciting* than seeing and Listening to someone who is actually *present.*

So be as human as you dare. Be authentic. Be vulnerable. Be open. Be real. Be you.

So, when you're talking about positive things, enjoy Disclosing:

"I'm excited about today. Because this project means a lot to me and the team I work with."

"To be honest, it's this insight, above all, that really makes me think we have an incredible opportunity..."

And, even when it comes to negative things, be bold in how honest you are:

"This, to be honest, was the darkest moment we had in the last six months. There were times when we wondered if, frankly, we shouldn't throw in the towel."

Honesty like this does nothing but add authenticity to a presentation or a talk.

And honesty about things that are potentially awkward is a great enabler...

"There's something slightly odd about talking to you today. Because, privately, I've been thinking you probably know more about much of this than I do..."

Admitting something was late, disappointing or wasn't great is good because it's honest, so the audience knows that you're authentic. But, if it's *purposeful*, it can be useful in another way, too: it enables you to be honest and direct about something you might otherwise be too shy or bashful to say:

"But there is something very specific I feel I can add to your thinking, because of the research we've been doing this year, which has shown us something that, potentially, might turn a lot of conventional thinking on its head."

Key thoughts

1. Capture your audience by *Describing* with powerful language. And *Navigate* us through the journey of the presentation.

2. *Check* and *Probe* to ask yourself questions that create the rhythms of a conversation.

3. *Listen* to your audience's reaction, then *Disclose* to create a rich authentic relationship with them.

Present yourself

There is no better recipe for successful presenting than these three words: *be here now*. It's a phrase that certainly can be applied to a significant conversation as much as doing a 30-minute talk. *Be* is such a great verb. It's not walk, talk, show, demonstrate, pretend, impress... it's be. Just *be* you. You are enough. And then there's the idea of *here*. To be honest, it doesn't matter *where* the here is. The important implication is that you are *fully* here. All of you. All of your mind. All of your attention. Bring your whole self to the physical space you're in. If that sounds a little obscure, just think of the times you've seen someone doing a presentation who's not fully *with* you. You can sense it almost immediately. They're doing something they could have done anywhere else. It might be vaguely interesting. But it's not compelling. And then, there's the *now*. Now is about the present. The moment. This day. This hour. This minute. So make sure you're yourself: conscious, aware and responsive to whatever is happening in the room. In every conversation that counts and in every presentation you give: Be. Here. Now.